MILITARY
LAND
ROVER
Development and in Service

MILITARY
LAND
ROVER
Development and in Service

Pat Ware

Ian Allan
PUBLISHING

Acknowledgements

This book could not have been produced without the invaluable assistance of the following people: David Fletcher, Librarian at the Tank Museum, Bovington, (TM) for sourcing original images, prints and documents from the archive; the Royal Arsenal West Historical Society (RA); Colin Glazebrook of Artco for finding rare and original Land Rover literature; Andrew Renwick of the Royal Air Force Museum (RAFM); the Imperial War Museum (IWM) for original FVRDE photographs; Paul Costen (PC), Bob Morrison (BM), Simon Thomson (ST) and Phillip Royal (PR) for their superb colour photographs; and James Taylor (JT) of Land Rover Enthusiast magazine for his encouragement and support.

Pat Ware
Woolwich,
May 2007.

Conceived and edited by Jasper Spencer-Smith
Jacket and page design: Crispin Goodall
Design and artwork: Nigel Pell
Scanning: JPS Ltd, Branksome, Poole, BH12 1DJ
Produced by JSS Publishing Limited,
PO. Box 6031, Bournemouth, BH1 9AT, England

First published 2007

ISBN (10) 0 7110 3189 4
ISBN (13) 978 0 7110 3189 0

Published by Ian Allan Publishing

An imprint of Ian Allan Publishing Ltd, Hersham, Surrey KT12 4RG
Printed by Ian Allan Printing Ltd, Hersham, Surrey KT12 4RG

Code 0706/C2

Visit the Ian Allan Publishing web site at:
www.ianallanpublishing.com

Title spread: Soldiers of the Heavy Machine Gun Platoon of the 1st Battalion Royal Irish Battle Group travel past one of the many burning oil wells, as they pass into Iraq. (WO2 Giles Penfold/Crown Copyright)

Cover: Men of 48 Field Squadron (Air Support) Royal Engineers and 42 Commando began operations at Camp Bastion, Helmand Province, Afghanistan, as part of Operation Herrick. (Sgt Rob Knight/Crown Copyright)

Contents

Introduction

Way back in 1948 the world was still recovering from a devastating war. In Britain steel was in short supply and the cry to industry was 'export or die'. Unable to gain sufficient supplies of steel for a new post-war motorcar and not quite ready to roll over and see his Rover Company die, Maurice Wilks suggested to his board that there might be some mileage to be gained from producing what was effectively a civilian version of the US-built Jeep as a post-war stopgap measure. Wilks had been using a war-surplus Jeep on his farm and thought that others might find such a machine to be equally useful. However, he can have had little idea of just how successful his Land Rover vehicle would become. And, were he still alive today, he would almost certainly be astonished to learn that the Land Rover, which his engineers had devised originally using the parts of yet another Jeep, remains in production some 60 years after introduction... and in a very recognisable form.

Wilks believed that the Land Rover could be used to pull a plough, drill holes for fence posts, run a welding set or pump, and deliver produce to market, and yet, at the same time, was sufficiently civilised to also serve as day-to-day transportation with equal facility. From these simple, agricultural beginnings the straightforward, no-nonsense Land Rover has gone on to become something of an automotive icon... one of just a handful of vehicles to have been admitted to this particular hall of fame.

But more than this, the Land Rover has also become a military icon, its service across the globe making it as readily identified as the Jeep.

From the original Series I, through the various incarnations of the Series II and III, to the Defender and the sophisticated Wolf, the versatile Land Rover has more than proved its capabilities in peace and war.

Like the Jeep before it, the Land Rover has been pressed into service in a myriad of roles. Special versions have been produced for long-range reconnaissance, tank busting, and as a mount for anti-aircraft missiles.

Alongside the more mundane cargo and general service vehicles there have also been special air-portable, amphibious and wading versions, armoured patrol vehicles, and gun tractors. The so-called Pink Panther, operated by Britain's SAS, remains the template for special forces machines capable of operating behind enemy lines for days on end... and the British Army's high-performance Wolf has been deployed in Afghanistan and Iraq.

Licence-built Land Rovers have been produced in Belgium, Australia, West Germany, Spain and Turkey, sometimes a little curious in appearance but nevertheless always recognisable as a Land Rover.

And the vehicle would almost certainly never have entered British Army service had it not been for the fact that the purpose-designed all-military Austin Champ project was in trouble. Cost over-runs, engineering problems and delivery difficulties encouraged the British War Office to buy Land Rovers... as an interim measure, just until the Champ was perfected.

Since 1948 the British Army has purchased thousands of Land Rovers with many others entering military service around the world... across Europe, Africa and the Middle East... even with the US Army.

Happily for the Land Rover enthusiast or historian, thousands of these vehicles still remain in service and hundreds of old warriors have been lovingly restored and preserved .

Left: Land Rover .
(X)

section one
Origins

1 | Origins

Although it has subsequently become a military icon in its own right, it is impossible to tell the story of the early military Land Rover without referring to two other vehicles. The first of these is the US-built Willys Jeep. Without the Jeep it would be safe to say that there would almost certainly be no Land Rover. The other is the Austin Champ, the ill-fated British attempt to produce a home-grown alternative to the Jeep.

Previous spread: Land Rover Series I mounted Royal Air Force Police from the Provost Headquarters (PHQ) provide escort for a high-ranking RAF officer at a Tactical Airforce (TAF) in what was then West Germany. *(RAFM)*

The Rover Company, which developed the mighty Land Rover, had an excellent pedigree. Its origins can be traced back to the 1860s when James Starley established the Coventry Sewing Machine Company with Josiah Turner. In 1868, the company started to produce French-designed velocipedes and the company name was changed to Coventry Machinists. Starley recruited his nephew John Kemp Starley but, within a year, he had set up his own company, Starley & Sutton at Meteor Works, Coventry. Widely acknowledged to be the father of the modern pedal cycle, it was John Starley who developed the so-called safety cycle, the design of which still forms the basis of the majority of modern bicycles. The name Rover was adopted in 1884. In 1896 Starley founded the Rover Cycle Company, capitalised at £150,000, and imported some Peugeot motorcycles in 1897 with a view to moving into the production of powered cycles.

Starley died in 1901 at the age of 46 but, in 1904, under a new managing director, Harry

Smyth, the company he founded continued to work on motorcycles, producing the first example in 1902. At the same time, the company also began to construct motorcars. Motorcycles were abandoned in 1905 and cycle production ceased in 1906 when the name was changed to the Rover Motor Company. More than 750 motorcars were produced in the first year of manufacture.

Rover cars were always aimed squarely at the affluent middle classes and, despite some serious setbacks during the depression years, the company established a reputation for building solid, dependable vehicles.

In 1928 a shareholders' action committee appointed Colonel Frank Searle to the board and he, in turn, employed Spencer B. Wilks, who had managed the Hillman Motor Company prior to its take-over by the Rootes Group, as General Manager. Wilks joined Rover in September 1929 and became Managing Director in 1933, and his acumen and foresight almost certainly saved

Rover from suffering the fate of so many of the smaller motor manufacturers. Wilks appointed his brother Maurice to the design department.

During World War Two the company abandoned vehicle production, concentrating instead on engine design. In 1943, Rover 'swapped' their jet engine project with Rolls-Royce, receiving in return manufacturing rights to the Meteor and Meteorite engines which were used to power tanks and large military vehicles.

When peace came in 1945, Rover had plans to supplement its luxury motorcars with a smaller, cheaper model known as the M type. Development work on the M type had started in 1944 but had been abandoned due to a shortage of steel and the British government's insistence that exports were to take priority.

Demand for the Meteor and Meteorite engines continued well into the 1960s but, without the M type, the company was facing something of a shortfall with no immediate prospect of how it could be filled. To make matters worse, it appeared that there was little export potential for the existing product range which meant that Rover was unlikely to receive adequate supplies of steel.

Birth of the Land Rover

There is no suggestion that the Land Rover, which ultimately more than filled the gap left by the M type, was anything more than a happy accident, but its story starts in 1946 when Maurice Wilks purchased a war-surplus Willys MB Jeep for use around his farm in North Wales.

Jeeps had been produced by Ford and Willys-Overland since 1941, with more than 625,000 examples manufactured by 1945. With the onset of peace surplus Jeeps were donated to the armies of the newly-liberated European nations, with the better examples being retained by US or British Forces. What remained, generally the most battle-worn examples, were disposed of on the civilian market. Perhaps not surprisingly, the Jeep owned by Wilks had already seen a fair bit of service.

Above: Produced by Ford and Willys-Overland, the standardised World War Two Jeep provided the pattern for all subsequent military vehicles of this type. *(PW)*

THE ALL-PURPOSE VEHICLE FOR THE FARM
THE UNIVERSAL 'Jeep'

One vehicle for almost endless uses on the farm and on the road. A paying investment that spreads its cost over many a job — as a runabout, truck, tractor and mobile power unit. Usable every day . . . every season of the year.

Handy as a farm runabout . . .

Practical as a farm pick-up truck . . .

Efficient as a farm tow-truck . . .

WILLYS EXPORT CORPORATION
TOLEDO 1, OHIO, U.S.A.

Cable Address:
"Willysexco"

Left and below:
The first Land Rover vehicle, seen here outside the factory, was constructed on a Jeep chassis and incorporated more than a few Jeep parts. Note the central steering position. *(RMC)*

When it started to wear out, and parts became difficult to find, Wilks started to wonder how it might be replaced.

It occurred to the Wilks brothers that, if Maurice had found the Jeep to be a useful vehicle around the farm, so might other farmers. Maurice resolved that Rover should build a Jeep-type utility vehicle, at least as a stopgap measure until Rover's post-war cars started to sell in reasonable numbers.

Excellent though this idea was, Maurice Wilks must have been perfectly well aware that he was not actually breaking new ground. Following the ending of military production of the MB, Willys-Overland had developed the so-called dual-purpose CJ-2A 'Universal Jeep', aiming it squarely at the rural farmer in the US. The CJ-2A went on sale in the US in July 1945 and, although it was subsequently offered for sale in France and the Netherlands, initially, there was no intention of looking for export orders.

The CJ-2A was offered with a variety of optional equipment which allowed it to be used for ploughing, sawing, spraying, welding, etc, as well as getting the farmer and his produce to town or market. Rover enthusiastically adopted the same approach.

It was mid-1947, two years after the launch of the CJ-2A, when work on what was soon described as the 'Landrover' project - note the use of one word - began at the company's Solihull factory. The small engineering team was led by Tom Barton; Gordon Bashford was responsible for the chassis, Robert Boyle was Chief Engineer, Arthur Goddard his assistant, and John Cullen was responsible for testing. The construction of the vehicle in Rover's jig shop was carried out under the direction of Geoffrey Savage.

Opposite: The idea of producing an all-purpose agricultural utility vehicle wasn't new… Willys-Overland had already put down a marker with the CJ-2A. *(RMC)*

Maurice Wilks' war surplus Jeep remained the role model for the project and, with little need to spend time on basic development, the team set to work to prepare outline drawings and to construct an engineering prototype which could be submitted for board approval. Some stories suggest that two more Jeeps were purchased and were driven and assessed before being pulled to pieces for parts. Others maintain that the prototype was constructed using components from Wilks' own Jeep.

Construction of the original prototype started in late September 1947 and was apparently completed in little more than two or three weeks. No suitable engine or gearbox was available so the 1,389cc unit from the pre-war Rover 10 motorcar was used. However, the most unusual feature of the prototype was the adoption of a central steering position intended to simplify production of vehicles for the domestic and European markets by making the driving position equally suitable for either side of the road. This must have presented the designers with a few difficulties as regards the operation of the steering gear and pedals.

The prototype was approved by the Rover board on 16 October 1947... and 50 pre-production models were commissioned with the intention of launching the vehicle at the 1948 Amsterdam Motor Show.

At the time, there was no intention of offering the vehicle to the military... although, of course, as things turned out military sales were crucial to the Land Rover's longevity.

The centre-steer prototype

Most Land Rover historians accept that the famous centre-steering prototype - effectively the forerunner of all subsequent Land Rovers - included 'elements' of the Jeep in its construction. Careful examination of a series of photographs of the prototype taken at Solihull on 15 October 1947 shows just how much Jeep there actually was in Land Rover number 1 - mainly that the chassis, along with most of the running gear, was pure World War Two Jeep.

The 1,389cc four cylinder water-cooled IOE engine of the Rover 10 was initially used to provide the power for the new vehicle but,

when this was found to be lacking, a new 1,595cc four cylinder water-cooled engine was used that was being developed for the new Rover P3. The four-speed gearbox was also said to have come from the Rover 10, but it was mated to the two-speed Spicer Model 18 transfer case taken from the Jeep. The four-wheel-drive system was permanently engaged, with the then-traditional Rover freewheel used to prevent undue torque stresses building-up in the drive-line. This meant that there was no engine braking available to assist in descending a steep incline.

Many Land Rover historians believe that a Rover 10 rear axle was fitted to the prototype, but the photographs show that the rear hubs are almost certainly those fitted on the standard fully-floating Spicer 23-2 unit of the Jeep. The front axle, too, has the distinctive early pattern driving flanges of the Jeep.

The Land Rover suspension was of the semi-elliptical springs type at both the front and rear, and retained the forged 'C'-shaped swinging shackles from the Jeep.

The bulkhead was moved further back on the chassis, which had the effect of placing the gear and transfer-box levers centrally in the floor area, and the steering wheel was placed in the centre of the full-width bench seat. The three-spoke wheel of the Jeep was replaced by a typical spoked Blumels unit, but the Ross T12 cam-and-lever steering box from the Jeep was retained. Despite the central steering position, the steering box remained in its original position on the inside face of the left-hand chassis member, and was connected to the steering column by means of a Reynolds roller chain, driving a sprocket. The fact that the Jeep axles remained in place suggests that Willys' curious axle-mounted bell crank was used to transmit the steering action to the front wheels.

The clutch pedal stayed where it was positioned by Willys, but the brake and accelerator pedals were relocated to the right. Since this effectively put the clutch where the brake would normally be, anyone driving the prototype had to keep alert.

The steel body tub of the Jeep was removed and discarded... but not before it had yielded various useful components.

Left: Champs and Land Rovers served beside one another in the British Army for around 10 years. *(PW)*

Rover's all-new open-sided body bore a passing resemblance to that of the Jeep, but the most notable difference was that the body panels were of 'Birmabright 2' aircraft-quality aluminium alloy, which was both easily obtained at the time and unrationed. Of equal importance, it was easy to work by hand and the selected body style required a minimum of working. Apart from the bonnet and wings most of the body panels were flat, particularly behind the scuttle where the framing was exposed. The characteristic upright folding windscreen, which appears to have employed the outer frame of the Jeep, was modified to fit the new scuttle and appeared to retain the windscreen-to-scuttle seal and over-centre locking catches of the original. The headlights were well-protected behind a wire mesh grille. Unlike the Jeep, there was a bottom-hinged folding tailgate.

The Rover body clearly had the hood frame, hood-frame supports, hood-frame stowage brackets, bonnet catches, and side handles of the Jeep.

The standard 16in two-piece 'combat' wheels of the Jeep were retained, and the length of the valve stem suggests that those dreadful hinged bead locks, designed to hold a deflated tyre in place, were also still in place. Some photographs

Above: The Rolls-Royce engined FV1801 Austin Champ was a British attempt at improving on the military Jeep. It proved to be costly, overweight and unreliable. *(IWM)*

show that the rims were shod with the standard 6.00x16 six-ply Goodyear 'bar grip' tyres as used on the Jeep, whilst others show Dunlop 'Trak-Grip' tyres.

A single seat was provided in the front, and as befits a utility vehicle, there was no rear seating.

Inside the body, the hinged lids of the Jeep tool boxes - the shape of the pressings suggesting Ford origin - were fitted to stowage boxes in the inner rear-wheel arches. On the dashboard, the speedometer, ammeter, and fuel and temperature gauges appear as though they may have been of US origin, although the switchgear and illumination are clearly British.

At the rear, the distinctive upswept angled ends of the Jeep's rearmost chassis cross member are clearly visible. The spare wheel is mounted inside the body, but is held in place by a modified Jeep retaining plate, and is almost certainly fitted on the Jeep bracket.

So the evidence shows that the first prototype of Britain's 'best 4x4 by far' was actually a miscellany of Willys and Rover parts.

Although almost certainly only one centre-steer prototype was constructed, there are persistent stories that a second chassis was built to test the feasibility of using the 1,595cc engine. Again the Jeep axles and hybrid transmission were used, but this chassis was apparently never fitted with bodywork.

Austin Champ

Work on what was eventually to become the Austin Champ had started during the closing years of Word War Two with the intention of producing a British Jeep.

Austin was asked to fit one of their own engines into a Jeep, and then to construct a prototype for an all-British replacement for the US vehicle. By 1944 their competitors, Nuffield Mechanisations, had produced a number of prototypes for such a vehicle, developing designs produced by the Fighting Vehicle Design Department (FVDD).

Powered by what may have been a 1,486cc Jowett water-cooled flat-four engine, the so-called Gutty featured a body of semi-stressed skin construction, independent suspension by longitudinal torsion bars, and a convertible steering position with duplicate pedal controls.

Right: The Champ's predecessor was the Wolseley Mudlark. It appeared in 1948, the same year as the Land Rover, and around 30 vehicles were built as mobile test beds. *(PW)*

The Gutty was not a resounding success and the designers at Nuffields were forced to go back to the drawing board. As part of the redesign process the vehicle was to adopt the standardised Rolls-Royce B40 four-cylinder engine, part of a family of similar four, six and eight-cylinder power units. Since the redesigned Gutty was not ready in sufficient time, some 34 Land Rovers were used as mobile test beds for the new Rolls-Royce engine.

By the time the vehicle emerged in 1948 as the Rolls-Royce-powered Wolseley FV1800 Mudlark, there was little to link it to the Gutty whose ungainly flat-panelled full-width body had been replaced by a rather more curvaceous design featuring separate front and rear mudguards. The independent suspension was retained, as was the stressed-skin design and, unusually, the vehicle offered five speeds in both directions by virtue of incorporating the forward/reverse gear in the transfer case.

In 1951, following the construction of 30 pre-production 'Mudlarks', the War Office issued a tender for a production contract for 15,000 similar vehicles. Although approached, Rover was obviously busy with the Land Rover, which had been on the market for three years and declined to become involved, instead offering Land Rovers at a saving of £3 million! In 1952 the contract went to Austin who started production at their Cofton Hackett factory in the West Midlands.

Sadly, the production vehicle, designated FV1801 and soon nicknamed 'Champ' after the civilian equivalent, had none of the Jeep's virtues. It was heavy, over-complex, and expensive. Problems quickly arose in service, with the rear axle proving especially vulnerable to failure.

By 1955 production of the FV1801 was complete, with the initial contract terminated prematurely after only 11,732 vehicles had been constructed. Each vehicle was said to have cost in the region of £1,100, at a time when a Land Rover cost around £550.

In 1948 the War Office had started buying Land Rovers as an interim measure whilst the FV1801 project was brought to fruition. The intention was always that the Champ would replace the Jeep in front-line service, with the Land Rover used as a 'behind the lines' back-up. As it happened things did not work out that way and the War Office realised that, although the Champ could perform various tricks which the Land Rover could not, perhaps some of these tricks were not actually necessary in peacetime.

For a period, the Jeep, Champ and the Land Rover served alongside one another in the British Army, almost as equals. But, at about the time that the Jeeps were finally withdrawn in the mid-1950s, the War Office decided to effectively abandon the Champ. There was to be no further production and, by August 1958, the Land Rover had been chosen as the British Army's standard $^1/_4$ ton-class tactical vehicle.

Thus, Rover's 'son of Jeep' replaced the expensive purpose-designed military vehicle and, unbeknown to those players involved in this drama from the beginning, a long and illustrious military career lay ahead… stretching more than 50 years into the future.

Above: One of the 48 pre-production Land Rovers showing the vehicle in more-or-less the form in which it was initially produced. The centre steering position has gone and both right- and left-hand drive vehicles formed part of this initial batch. (RMC)

section two
The Major Models

2.1 | Series 1

With board approval of the centre-steering prototype secured, work started on the planned 50 pre-production vehicles. The first 25 had been produced by late 1947, and most of the remainder followed in early 1948. All of the pre-production models were fitted with the larger engine which had been intended for the Rover 60 saloon car and, most notably, were without the centre steering position.

Previous spread: Members of No. 4001 Armoured Car Flight of the RAF Regiment on patrol in the Canal Zone, Egypt in 1953. The Series I Land Rover is followed by a Humber Mk III airfield-defence armoured car. *(RAFM)*

Although only 48 of these vehicles were eventually constructed, as planned Rover did launch the Series I at the Amsterdam Motor Show in April 1948. In papers submitted to the board for approval of the project it had been envisaged that sales might perhaps reach 50, or maybe even 100, a week but significant orders started coming in for the new vehicle almost from the moment it went on sale. Full-scale production started in July 1948, and what had originally been seen as a stopgap measure became crucially important.

In 1949, the first full year of production, total sales exceeded 8,000, with production of the Land Rover equal to that of the company's motorcars. By 1951 sales had doubled, and Land Rover production was exceeding car production by a ratio of two to one.

It is worth remembering that despite Jeep ancestry, Rover had never seen the Land Rover as a military vehicle. Clearly others had different ideas and, in 1948, the Ministry of Supply had

acquired two of the pre-production Land Rovers for trials, one of which was a left-hand drive model (chassis number L29) and the other right-hand drive (R30).

It is not difficult to see why the Land Rover might have been considered a god-send since the Army was in trouble with its utility vehicles. The remaining stock of World War Two-vintage Jeeps was rapidly ageing and the FV1800 Champ project was proceeding far more slowly than had been anticipated and with also considerable increases in cost. A critical shortage of utility vehicles was looming and the Land Rover appeared to offer a short-term solution. Land Rovers could not only solve the immediate problem but, once deliveries of the 'combat' Champ got underway, with its similar payload and outline design, the Land Rover could remain in service as a lower-cost partner. Less than 12 months later, in 1949, G. P. Walsh, Deputy Director, Weapons Development, grudgingly wrote that 'the Land Rover would meet the requirements (for the so-called utility range)...

but it is considered that a Jeep with relaxed specification is required in order to maintain some standardisation... providing the cost approaches that of the Land Rover'.

The two pre-production Land Rovers were delivered to the Fighting Vehicles Development Establishment (FVDE) in June 1948, and were put through the standard automotive trials at the Chertsey and Bagshot Heath proving grounds. At the end of the trials a number of possible improvements were suggested, but it was generally felt that the Land Rover would form a useful addition to the War Office fleet and, in one of a series of monthly bulletins describing developments in new equipment, FVDE informed the user services that 'a Land Rover vehicle has been procured for trials in view of the possibility of a number of these vehicles being used by the Services as an interim measure'.

Almost immediately, an additional 20 vehicles were ordered from the initial production run for 'further evaluation'.

Production

Meanwhile, production of the Series I had begun in earnest in July 1948 at the Lode Lane site, the Solihull 'shadow' factory which Rover had converted to motorcar production after the end

Above: Left-hand drive pre-production vehicle, probably chassis number L29 as supplied to FVRDE. *(IWM)*

Above: A radio equipped Series I of the Trucial Oman Scouts in the desert near Sharjah, February 1962. *(IWM)*

of the war. Just as the pilot, (pre-production) models, had differed from the prototype, changes were also made to the first production examples.

The 80in (2.03m) wheelbase remained, as did the aluminium-alloy body, but the chassis was no longer galvanised. Changes were made to the layout of the exhaust, and the wheels were no longer of the split-rim 'combat' type, but were of conventional one-piece well-base design.

The doors were strengthened, and the hinges and handles were improved; the design of the seats was modified. The colour of the body was standardised as Sage Green, a colour which (rumour has it) derived from war-surplus RAF cockpit interior paint. When military contracts began to dominate the production lines from mid-1949, the colour was changed again to the standard military Deep Bronze Green regardless of whether the vehicle was intended for military or civilian use, since it seemed easier to paint all of the vehicles in the same colour. It was not until 1954 that the familiar blue and grey finishes were made available to civilians.

It had originally been intended that a hood and side-screens would be optional extras. This idea was rapidly abandoned but, at first, there

was only a short canvas tilt available to cover the cab area. Subsequently there was a choice of a full tilt cover, which also covered the cargo area, a full-length metal hardtop, or a metal cab. The spare wheel was carried upright inside the load bed, or flat, on the optional bonnet mount.

The retail price of the vehicle was £450, rising to £540 in October, 1948.

Development

Development continued at a pace during the first five years of the Land Rover's existence, and small, but often significant, improvements were made to many components and assemblies. Since the vehicles supplied to the Ministry of Supply were, to all intents and purposes, identical to their commercial counterparts, these improvements also found their way into the government vehicles.

In mid-1948 the rear axle ratio was changed when the unit originally designed for the Rover 12 was replaced by the axle intended for the P3 saloon. In 1950 the gearbox was also changed for a similar reason and, during October of 1950 after some 1,500 units had been produced, the permanent four-wheel drive and freewheel

facility was dropped with the transmission being replaced by the more usual selectable two or four-wheel-drive configuration. Along with this change the gearlever was conventionally mounted directly into the gearbox, rather than being attached to the body. At the same time the dash was changed to a pressed-metal design.

Early examples were fitted with Girling Hydrastatic self-adjusting brakes, but these were soon discontinued in favour of a more conventional Girling design. Early in production the brake fluid reservoir was moved from the scuttle to the seat box, with the seat box design being modified. The shock absorbers were changed so that both front and rear units were the same type.

In 1950 the headlamps, which had already been increased in size, were no longer covered by the wire-mesh grille. A year later, in 1951, the sidelamps were moved from their curious bulkhead position to a more conventional wing mount, and the grille was modified to the distinctive inverted 'T' design.

The 1,595cc engine had been replaced by a more powerful 1,997cc version in August 1951. Although the new engine was essentially a bored-

out version of the same unit, it offered an additional 2bhp, with a useful 25% increase in low-speed torque. In 1953 the 1,997cc unit was replaced by a re-engineered version based on that used in the P4 Rover 60 saloon car. The two engines were outwardly similar, but the new unit had equally-spaced, rather than 'siamesed', bores giving better cooling characteristics.

The wheelbase was increased to 86in (2.18m) in 1954 and, at the same time, Rover also

Above: Early FV18001 80in Series I fitted with what was possibly a sample factory hardtop. *(PR [top] PW [below])*

windscreen hinges placed higher on the bulkhead. The door handles were moved outside the body in 1951, and recessed into the doors in 1954.

The 107in (2.72m) wheelbase dimension was upped to 109in (2.77m) in 1957, at which time the 86in (2.18m) wheelbase was increased to 88in (2.24m). The extra 2in (5cm) were required to accommodate the new overhead valve engine… although first put to good use when the new diesel engine was fitted.

Various users, including the War Office, had experimented with diesel power, usually choosing Perkins engines, so it should have come as no surprise when an optional four-cylinder, direct-injection 1,997cc diesel was offered for the Series I in 1957.

The military Series I

At the end of 1949 the Ministry of Supply had acquired two production Land Rovers. These were subjected to further military trials to check that the modifications which had been made

launched the long-wheelbase 107in (2.72m) version. Among other changes, the 86in (2.18m) vehicles were fitted with a new, larger instrument panel and new rear lights. The bonnet catches were moved nearer to the windscreen with the

following the report on the pre-production machines, were satisfactory.

On 5 January 1950, after the first vehicle had run approximately 10,000 miles (16,093km), a preliminary report was issued with a number of minor failures and difficulties noted. The only real difficulty involved the water pump, which had given continual trouble before finally being replaced with a modified unit. The engine was stripped and measurements were taken of the cylinder bores - the wear was determined to be 'well within acceptable limits'. It was stated that the condition of the vehicle was 'good'. It compared favourably with the pre-production machines, and it was said that the modifications introduced as a result of the first series of trials 'had so far proved effective'. The trial was resumed.

The rear axle of the second vehicle failed before 20,000 miles (32,186km) had been covered, apparently as a result of poor setting-up during production. Five teeth had sheared off the crown wheel resulting in damage to the pinion in the differential. The differential was replaced and the trials continued.

On 8 September 1950, A. E. Masters, FVDE Chief Engineer, issued the final report on the second vehicle, which had covered 20,356 miles (32,759km) including some 4,500 miles (7,241km) across country. Replacements during the trials included one set of spark plugs, a water pump, gearbox selector spring, rear differential, four 'Silentbloc' suspension bushes, a rear spring and bump rubbers, and six tyres. The engine was stripped for internal examination, and the degree of wear suggested that life to a first major overhaul would be in the order of 20,000 miles (32,186km) - although it is unclear whether this meant another 20,000 miles (32,186km) or whether the engine was actually already requiring an overhaul.

In its final conclusion the report stated quite categorically that 'the production type Land Rover as supplied to the Army has a satisfactory degree of reliability, especially in view of the fact that it is a standard vehicle in commercial production'.

In May 1950, not long after FVDE had initiated these tests, the Royal Air Force (RAF) had taken delivery of a batch of 100 Series I cargo

Above: Hardtops, which were not offered to civilians until 1950, were rare in military service in the early years. This vehicle, in RAF service, is towing a special trailer for carrying the WE177 air-dropped nuclear weapon carried by Tornado aircraft. The weapon shown is a dummy round. *(RAFM)*

Right: The long-wheelbase 107in (later 109in) cargo Series I was not common in military service. A patrol of the Trucial Oman Scouts take up defensive positions around their vehicles in the desert, near Sharjah, February 1962. *(IWM)*

Below: Standard Series I GS cargo variant. For a period all Land Rovers were painted in the military Deep Bronze Green regardless of customer. *(PW)*

vehicles, almost certainly the first military Land Rovers to be delivered in quantity. Despite some initial uncertainty as to exactly how many Land Rovers might eventually be required, the Ministry of Supply also issued a contract for 1,910 similar vehicles for use by the Army.

By June 1951 3,674 examples had been ordered, and the requirement for the next three financial years was projected as 600 vehicles for 1951/52, 900 for 1952/53, and 1,000 for 1953/54, at an estimated price of £625 each. In all some 5% of total output, representing 15,000 vehicles, went to the Ministry of Supply over the 10-year life of the Series I.

Although various contracts called for a degree of light modification to better suit the vehicle to its military service, these Land Rovers were essentially standard civilian vehicles. At this stage there was never any attempt made at producing an exclusively military Land Rover. Such modifications as were specified generally concerned items such as wheels and the provision of lashing eyes, reinforced rear cross-member and towing pintle, also changes to electrical and lighting equipment. However it is worth noting that before accepting the new 2-litre engine for military use, the Fighting Vehicles Research & Development Establishment

(FVRDE), as it had become by that time, insisted on a thorough trial of 20,000 miles (32,186km) at their testing ground at Chertsey in Surrey.

A number of cargo vehicles were converted to the communications role in Army workshops, and some of these were also subsequently retro-fitted with a 24V negative-earth electrical system. The changes involved the use of a metal radio table which was installed across the rear of the vehicle behind the front seats, the installation of supplementary batteries to power the radio equipment, and the use of a screened electrical system. This used a different type of coil and distributor as well as screened spark plugs.

The 107in (2.72m) long-wheelbase pick-up truck was trialled at FVRDE soon after it was announced in 1954 but, as far as is known, none entered service with the British Army. Of course, this chassis also formed the basis of the special ambulances (see page 104). Elsewhere, others clearly believed that the long-wheelbase pick-up had some military application, for 12 of these

107in (2.72m) pick-ups with truck cabs, and described as 'field unit vehicles', were purchased by the Irish Defence Force (IDF) and used as towing vehicles for anti-tank and mortar units. They were also used as cable layers and communications vehicles; two similar vehicles

Above: Short-wheelbase Series I adapted as a signals line-layer. *(RA)*

Top: Standard short-wheelbase Series I GS vehicle from the first large contract which called for almost 2000 vehicles in 1949. *(RA)*

Above: The long-wheelbase GS vehicle appeared in 1954. This example was photographed at FVRDE whilst undergoing trials. *(RA)*

were supplied in 1958 with the extended 109in (2.77m) wheelbase.

In Britain, the Land Rover was still in service alongside the Austin Champ, although most of the Jeeps had already been retired. The War Office still insisted that there was no intention of abandoning the Champ, stating that the two vehicles could continue to operate alongside one another. But cracks were clearly forming in the façade and, in 1956, the Wilks brothers had attended a meeting at FVRDE, to discuss the future of the Land Rover in military service. By that time, the production run for the Champ was complete and the vehicle was proving itself to be unreliable. In August 1958, the Director, Weapons Development wrote that '40% of the 1/4 ton vehicles in the British Army are Land Rovers... [and that the Land Rover] has become the standard 1/4 ton tactical and utility vehicle...'.

He went on to say that 'the War Office has every confidence in the Land Rover as a tactical front line vehicle'.

Within eight years all of the Champs were gone... either handed over to the Territorial Army or sold at auction. Sadly for Austin, the civilian version of the vehicle was no more successful, selling only in very small numbers.

Outside of Great Britain, the Series I had also entered service with the Irish Defence Force, the Netherlands Army and, in locally-constructed versions, with the West German border guards and the Belgian Army; these latter vehicles are dealt with separately.

The Series I was superseded by the Series II in April 1958 and, in just 10 years, the essentially civilian Land Rover, initially purchased as an 'interim' measure, had replaced the totally military Champ.

Series I 'utility'

Something of an aberration occurred in 1957, when Land Rover produced a unique 4x2 version of the 88in (2.24m) Rover Mk 5 for the British Army.

The vehicle, which was almost certainly developed by Army workshops, was considered to be a 'car' and was intended for use as a general utility vehicle. Although externally indistinguishable from normal 4x4 Land Rovers, there was no front axle drive, a cover was fitted on the transfer box output housing, with a lock-out on the transfer box to prevent selection of the low-ratio gears; and the front axle itself was a simple tube design, with the hub carriers welded to the ends. Deliveries started in 1957, and the Army received 655 cargo vehicles and 20 station wagons.

Roles

The Land Rover was adapted to a variety of military roles including, for example, signals line layer, helicopter starting, lighting maintenance unit, MOBAT tow vehicle, communications truck, command vehicle, gun platform (see page 136), airfield fire-crash-rescue (see page 104), etc.

With the addition of a snorkel and the application of suitable waterproofing, the vehicle could be made amphibious.

Technical specifications
Series I GS vehicles; 1948 to 1958
Typical nomenclature: truck, 1/4 ton, cargo, GS, 4x4; FV18001; Rover Mks 1, 2, 3.

Engine: Land Rover; four cylinders; 1,595cc or 1,997cc; petrol; overhead inlet valves, side exhaust; power output, 41-52bhp at 4,000rpm; torque, 80-101 lbf/ft at 2,500rpm.
Transmission: 4F1Rx2; part-time 4x4 (full-time 4x4 on early models, with freewheel).
Steering: recirculating ball, worm and nut.
Suspension: live axles on multi-leaf semi-elliptical springs; hydraulic double-acting telescopic shock absorbers.
Brakes: hydraulic; drums all-round.
Construction: welded box-section steel chassis; steel-framed aluminium-panelled body.
Electrical system: 12V.

Dimensions
Length, (short wheelbase), 132-145in (3.35-3.68m); (long wheelbase), 170in (4.32m).
Width, 62in (1.58m).
Height (open vehicles, top fitted), 70-76in (1.78-1.93m); (closed vehicles), 72in (1.83m).
Wheelbase, 80, 86, 88, 107 & 109in (2.03, 2.18, 2.24, 2.72 & 2.77m).
Ground clearance, 8.5in (21.6cm).
Weight, (short wheelbase), 2,721lb (1,234.25kg) unladen, 4,094lb (1,857.04kg) laden; (long wheelbase) 3,240lb (1,469.7kg) unladen, 4,899lb (2,222.19kg) laden.

Performance
Average speed, (road) 45mph (72.42kph); (cross country) 15mph (24.14kph).
Range of action, 220 miles (354km).
Approach angle, 46°;
Departure angle, 37°.
Fording depth, 24in (61cm).

Military mark numbers
All military Series I Land Rovers were assigned 'mark' numbers according to major variations from the original specification. These numbers, which were not used by Rover, indicated only the basic chassis type:
- Rover Mk 1 - original Series I cargo vehicle, with 1,595cc F-head engine.
- Rover Mk 2 - standard, late-production 80in (2.03m) Series I, with 1,997cc F-head engine.
- Rover Mk 3 - 86in (2.18m) wheelbase Series I, with either the 43bhp or 52bhp 1,997cc F-head engine.
- Rover Mk 4 - long-wheelbase (107 or 109in [2.72 or 2.77m]) cargo vehicle or heavy utility (station wagon); also used as the basis for a mountain rescue, or special ambulance.
- Rover Mk 5 - 88in (2.24m) wheelbase Series I, including the 4x2 'utility'.

The mark number referred only to the basic chassis, the individual vehicle type was designated by 'FV' number.

FV numbers
- FV18001 Truck, 1/4 ton, cargo, GS, 4x4; Rover Mks 1, 2, 3
- FV18002 Truck, 1/4 ton, cargo, GS, armoured, 4x4; Rover Mk 3
- FV18003 Van, 10cwt, airfield lighting maintenance, 4x4; Rover Mk 3
- FV18004 Car, heavy utility, LWB, 4x4; Rover Mk 4
- FV18005 Truck, 1/4 ton, ambulance, special, GS, 4x4; Rover Mk 4
- FV18006 Truck, 1/4 ton, SAS, GS, 4x4; Rover Mks 3, 5
- FV18007 Truck, 1/4 ton, cargo, GS, 4x4; Rover Mks 4, 5; or Car, 1/4 ton, utility, GS, 4x2; Rover Mk 5
- FV18008 Truck, 1/4 ton, ambulance, two stretchers, GS, 4x4; Rover Mk 4
- FV18009 Truck, 1/4 ton, MOBAT towing, GS; Rover Mk 5
- FV18010 Truck, 1/4 ton, guards paratroops, GS, 4x4; Rover Mks 3, 5

Above: A British Army convoy of Series II Land Rovers prepares to leave for a patrol along the Aden/Yemen frontier, June 1959. *(IWM)*

2.2 | Series II and IIA

Production of the Series I continued for a decade, until April 1958, when it was replaced by the revised Series II. Although the vehicle was recognisably still a Land Rover, Rover's in-house styling team, under the direction of David Bache, had made various external changes to its appearance.

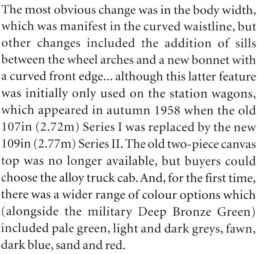

The most obvious change was in the body width, which was manifest in the curved waistline, but other changes included the addition of sills between the wheel arches and a new bonnet with a curved front edge... although this latter feature was initially only used on the station wagons, which appeared in autumn 1958 when the old 107in (2.72m) Series I was replaced by the new 109in (2.77m) Series II. The old two-piece canvas top was no longer available, but buyers could choose the alloy truck cab. And, for the first time, there was a wider range of colour options which (alongside the military Deep Bronze Green) included pale green, light and dark greys, fawn, dark blue, sand and red.

However, the changes were certainly not entirely visual and the Series II was a genuinely improved vehicle. Under the bonnet, was a new overhead valve 2,286cc 77bhp engine... although stocks of the old 2-litre unit had to be used up first and, initially, only the 109in (2.77m) models were fitted with the new power unit. The new engine was derived from the diesel unit which had been announced in 1957, being fitted with different pistons and a gas-flowed (improved effciency) cylinder head; the cylinder liners used on the diesel unit were also omitted which helps to explain the increase in capacity.

The increased overall width also allowed the track to be increased, which had the bonus effect of reducing the turning circle. New, softer springs and redesigned dampers provided improvements to the ride, whilst the rear springs were also relocated to allow greater suspension travel.

Other improvements included redesigned door hinges, new lighting arrangements, and the use of pendant pedals to replace the old 'through-the-floor' design.

The Series II continued in production for just three years. Some 28,371 vehicles were produced in 1958/59, rising to 35,148 in 1960/61, when it was replaced by the Series IIA. In November 1959 a milestone was reached

Above and left:
The Series II, launched in 1958, entered military service in both long and short-wheelbase forms; it can easily be recognised by the additional width on the body sides. *(IWM)*

with the 25,000th vehicle rolling off the production line.

The Series IIA appeared in September 1961, and remained in production until September 1971. The most obvious change was the replacement of the old 1,997cc diesel engine with a more powerful 2,286cc unit. Rover also exploited a loophole in the UK purchase tax legislation, offering a 12-seater station wagon on the domestic market alongside the standard 10-seater, although this was of little concern to the military.

Between 1961 and 1966, production continued to grow, with the 500,000th vehicle produced in April 1966. During this period there were virtually no further changes made, although Rover did introduce the first forward-control model in 1962. The vehicle was trialled by the War Office, but no volume purchases were made.

On the corporate front, Rover found it increasingly hard to compete as an independent and, in 1967, was purchased by the rapidly-expanding Leyland Group.

A six-cylinder engine option was introduced in April of that year, continuing in production until it was replaced by the 3.5-litre V8 in the Series III of 1980... although the British Army continued to rely on the four-cylinder 2,286cc engine for some considerable time. A number of other changes were made to the Series IIA during this period, the most obvious of which was the repositioning of the headlamps in the front panels of the wings, initially to meet changing legislation in the Netherlands, Belgium and Luxembourg... or perhaps, as some sources claim, the US. Other changes included the use of a Zenith carburettor in place of the original Solex unit, a negative earth electrical system, and some tidying up of switchgear and the minor controls on the fascia.

The Series IIA was replaced by the Series III in 1971, by which time 500,000 vehicles had been produced for export alone. BMC had merged with Jaguar in 1966 to form the short-lived British Motor Holdings (BMH). In 1968, BMH and Leyland came together to form what was to be the ill-fated British Leyland Motor Corporation.

The military Series II/IIA

Through the life of the Series II and IIA, Rover continued to supply vehicles to the War Office, the Royal Navy and the Air Ministry. Other armies were also starting to take notice and, in 1959, the Australian Army standardised on the Land Rover, as did the Swiss Army a year later; the Irish Defence Force continued to buy Land Rovers in small numbers, taking delivery of both Series II and IIA models in both long and short-wheelbase form. By 1963, the Land Rover was in service with the armed forces of 26 countries around the world.

It is still worth remembering that the Land Rover was not a military vehicle in the sense that it had been designed by, or on behalf of, the British War Office... unlike other vehicles in British Army service, very few of the changes which took place to the design and specification were initiated by the military authorities.

Such changes as were made on behalf of the military, were relatively superficial, often amounting to little more than the use of longer spring hangers to enable the use of larger two-piece wheels and military tyres, and strengthened axles. Other changes included the addition of a military tow hitch on a reinforced rear cross member, the use of a military-pattern trailer socket, twin fuel tanks, lashing eyes, and double-height pusher bumpers at the front. Some vehicles were fitted with an oil cooler.

Above: Short wheelbase Series II and trailer being lifted by a Bristol Belvedere twin-rotor helicopter. *(RAFM)*

Opposite page: Long and short-wheelbase Series IIs showing open and closed configurations. The vehicle in the bottom picture is fitted for radio (FFR). *(PW)*

Above: Unusual van-bodied Series II of unknown origin and purpose. It was photographed at FVRDE. *(IWM)*

The Army finally abandoned the use of split-rim wheels in 1968 with the adoption of a new design of well-base rims, which were also standardised for civilian models.

Although the British services were generally not interested in specifying diesel power, experiments were conducted during the early 1960s with multi-fuel engines which ultimately proved themselves to be unreliable and also lacking in power. Diesel-engined vehicles were supplied to the Irish Defence Force.

As with the Series I, purpose-designed military variants were generally not supplied by the factory and were either constructed in Army workshops or, as in the case of the Special Air Service (SAS) 'Pink Panthers', the work was contracted out by the military. However, there was one notable exception and that was in vehicles intended for the communications role.

A number of Mk 3 and Mk 5 Series I vehicles had already been used in this way, some even being retro-fitted with a 24V negative-earth electrical system. With the appearance of the Series IIA, vehicles were supplied for the first time from the factory in what was described as FFR (fitted for radio) condition. As manufactured, all Mk 8, 9, 10 and 11 FFR vehicles were fitted with a 24V negative-earth screened electrical system with either a 40Ah or 90Ah alternator. The electrical system was fully screened to prevent interference when the radio sets were in operation. There was provision made for attaching the standard antenna base on a rod mount on either side of the body rear and tailored apertures were provided in the hood to allow the aerial leads to be passed out to the antenna mount. The front wings were strengthened to receive the box-like aerial tuner unit (ATU).

Inside the vehicle, additional wiring and junction boxes were fitted to facilitate connection of the radios to the vehicle's electrical system and to allow aerials to be connected to the radio sets. A sliding wooden table top was installed behind the front seats, spanning across the wheel-arch boxes.

The table top was drilled to allow installation of two radio carriers, and Dexion slotted angle was fitted above the table to provide a secure route for cables and an attachment point for control equipment. A single radio operator's seat was installed in the rear of the short-wheelbase vehicles, facing inwards, with two such seats provided in the long-wheelbase equivalent. The Mk 9 also included a short radio table, in either the left or right-hand rear corner, to allow the installation of a third radio set.

Two additional 100Ah batteries were required to power the radio, and these were installed in a carrier beneath the table. A power take-off system allowed the batteries to be float-charged whilst the vehicle's engine was running. A pair of ammeters was installed to the left of the instrument panel to measure the charging current in the circuits of the radio and vehicle battery systems.

All of this meant that the vehicle was simply ready for the easy installation of radio equipment, not that it necessarily had such equipment installed.

Series II 'utility'

Small numbers of Series II 4x2 chassis were supplied to the British Army in 1958, when some 275 vehicles of the 88in (2.24m) Mk 6 cargo type were constructed with rear-wheel drive only.

Roles

As time went on, the services seemed to find more and more roles for the Land Rover. An enormous variety of specialised vehicles were constructed on the basic Series II and IIA chassis, generally in Army workshops. Typical military uses included aircraft crash-rescue (see page 116), signals and communications, line-laying, vehicle servicing, gun platform (page 136), helicopter starting, radar calibration unit, mine detection, carrier for missile computers and test equipment, and also utility and command vehicles.

With the addition of a snorkel and the application of suitable waterproofing, the vehicle could be made amphibious.

Above and right:
Special bodies were often fitted for specific roles for which the standard vehicle might not have been suitable. *(TM [top] RA [right])*

Technical specifications
Series II and IIA GS vehicles; 1958 to 1971
Typical nomenclature: truck, 1/4 ton, cargo, GS, 4x4; FV18021; Rover 6.

Engine: Land Rover; four cylinders; 2,286cc; overhead valves; petrol; power output, 77bhp at 4,250rpm; torque, 124 lbf/ft at 2,500rpm.
Transmission: 4F1Rx2; part-time 4x4.
Steering: recirculating ball, worm and nut.
Suspension: live axles on multi-leaf semi-elliptical springs; hydraulic double-acting telescopic shock absorbers.
Brakes: hydraulic; drums all-round.
Construction: welded box-section steel chassis; steel-framed aluminium-panelled body.
Electrical system: 12V or 24V.

Dimensions
Length, (short wheelbase), 142in (3.61m); (long wheelbase), 175in (4.45m).
Width, 64in (1.26m).
Height, (open vehicles, top fitted), 78in (1.98m). (closed vehicles), 81in (2.05m).
Wheelbase, 88 or 109in (2.24 or 2.77m).
Ground clearance, 8.5 or 9in (21.6 or 22.9cm), according to tyre equipment.
Weight (short wheelbase), 2,900lb (1,315.44kg) unladen, 4,453lb (2,020kg) laden; (long wheelbase) 3,294lb (1,494.16kg) unladen, 5,905lb (2,678.5kg) laden.

Performance
Maximum speed, (road) 65mph (104.6kph); (cross country) 30mph (48.3kph).
Range of action, 280-360 miles (335-579km).
Approach angle, 47°;
Departure angle, 29°.
Fording depth, 20in (50.8cm).

Military mark numbers
Like the military Series I, individual 'mark' numbers were assigned to the vehicles according to major variations from the original specification:

- Rover 6 - 88in (2.24m) wheelbase Series II cargo vehicle.
- Rover 7 - 109in (2.77m) wheelbase Series II, either supplied as a cargo vehicle, heavy utility or special ambulance.
- Rover 8 - 88in (2.24m) Series IIA; a suffix '/1' (eg, 'Rover 8/1') indicated that the rear differential and half-shafts were strengthened; suffix '/2' indicated that they were standard.
- Rover 9 - 109in (2.77m) cargo vehicle, heavy utility or special ambulance; again, suffixed '/1' or '/2' to indicate the presence of strengthened axles.
- Rover 10 - 88in (2.24m) upgraded Series IIA.
- Rover 11 - 109in (2.77m) upgraded Series IIA.

The mark number referred only to the basic chassis, the individual vehicle type was designated by 'FV' number.

FV numbers

- FV18021 Truck, 1/4 ton, cargo, GS, 4x4; Rover 6
- FV18022 Truck, 1/4 ton, airfield lighting maintenance, 4x4; Rover 6
- FV18023 Truck, 1/4 ton, helicopter starting, GS, 4x4; Rover 6
- FV18024 Truck, 1/4 ton, cargo, 4x4; Rover 8/1, 8/2
- FV18025 Truck, 1/4 ton, cargo, FFR, 4x4; Rover 8/1, 8/2
- FV18031 Truck, 1/4 ton, cargo, FFR-24V, 4x4; Rover 10
- FV18032 Truck, 1/4 ton, cargo, FFR-12V, 4x4; Rover 10
- FV18041 Truck, 3/4 ton, cargo, GS, 4x4; Rover 7
- FV18042 Car, utility, heavy, 4x4; Rover 7, 9
- FV18043 Truck, 3/4 ton, ambulance, 2 stretcher, mountain rescue, GS, 4x4; Rover 7
- FV18044 Truck, 3/4 ton, ambulance, 2 stretcher, GS, 4x4; Rover 7
- FV18045 Truck, 3/4 ton, WOMBAT, 4x4; Rover 7
- FV18046 Truck, 3/4 ton, sensitivity test, SAGW number 2, 4x4; Rover 7
- FV18047 Truck, 3/4 ton, fire-fighting, airfield crash rescue, 4x4; Rover 9, 11
- FV18048 Truck, 3/4 ton, computer, 4x4; Rover 7
- FV18049 Truck, 3/4 ton, computer, SSGW number 1, 4x4; Rover 7
- FV18050 Truck, 3/4 ton, fuse test equipment, SSGW number 1, 4x4; Rover 7
- FV18051 Truck, 3/4 ton, mine detector, 4x4; Rover 7
- FV18051 Truck, airportable, general purpose (APGP), scheme A; Rover 9
- FV18052 Truck, 3/4 ton, cargo, 4x4; Rover 9/1, 9/2
- FV18053 Truck, 3/4 ton, cargo, FFR, 4x4; Rover 9/1, 9/2
- FV18054 Truck, 3/4 ton, ambulance, 2/4 stretcher, 4x4; Rover 7
- FV18055 Truck, 3/4 ton, ambulance, 2/4 stretcher, mountain rescue, 4x4; Rover 7
- FV18061 Truck, 3/4 ton, cargo, 4x4; Rover 9, 11 (also Series 3)
- FV18061 Truck, airportable, general purpose (APGP), scheme B; Rover 9
- FV18062 Truck, 3/4 ton, cargo, FFR-24V, 4x4; Rover 9, 11 (also Series 3)
- FV18063 Truck, 3/4 ton, gun radar calibration, 4x4; Rover 9, 11 (also Series 3)
- FV18064 Truck, 3/4 ton, SAS, 4x4; Rover 9, 11
- FV18065 Truck, 3/4 ton, ambulance, 2 stretcher, 4x4; Rover 9, 11 (also Series 3)
- FV18066 Truck, 3/4 ton, ambulance, 2 stretcher, mountain rescue, 4x4; Rover 9, 11 (also Series 3)
- FV18067 Truck, 3/4 ton, ambulance, 2/4 stretcher Mk 2, 4x4; Rover 9, 11 (also Series 3)
- FV18068 Truck, 3/4 ton, ambulance, 2/4 stretcher Mk 2, mountain rescue, 4x4; Rover 9, 11 (also Series 3)
- FV18069 Truck, 3/4 ton, fire fighting, airfield crash rescue, tactical, 4x4; Rover 9, 11
- FV18070 Truck, 3/4 ton, radar set, truck mounted, 4x4; Rover 9, 11

2.3 | Series III

By the time the production of the Series IIA came to an end in 1971, the vehicle was beginning to look very long in the tooth. In the mid-1960s Rover had commissioned a radical redesign, at least on paper, but had lacked the funding to proceed. At the end of the decade the company was citing market research which claimed that customers were looking for a modernisation package rather than any quantum leaps forward.

   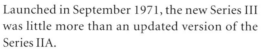  

Launched in September 1971, the new Series III was little more than an updated version of the Series IIA.

Many would argue that the new all-synchromesh gearbox, combined with a reduced low-ratio gear in the transfer box, was the most significant change, albeit the gearbox had already been trialled, unannounced in the Series IIA, and anyway proved to be weaker than the version it replaced. Others might have pointed to the prominence of the rather unattractive plastic radiator grille! Under the bonnet, the dynamo was replaced by an alternator, and the battery was taken out from under the seats and positioned under the bonnet. Other changes included a new diaphragm clutch, improved brakes with optional servo assistance, strengthened stub axles and a heavy-duty Salisbury rear axle with improved half-shafts. This latter upgrade was initially reserved for the six-cylinder models, but became standard fitment on all long-wheelbase chassis in 1972.

Visually, there was little, apart from that radiator grille, and new door hinges, which protruded rather less than the originals, to distinguish the new model.

Inside, it was another matter. The dashboard was completely redesigned, positioning the instruments in front of the driver and incorporating a stowage locker. There was also a new steering wheel on a lockable column, the heating system was improved… and there was even provision for a radio!

Overdrive was offered as a standard option from August 1974, giving an improvement in fuel consumption of around 3mpg (1.1km/l).

Rover, faced with ever-rising costs and a high rate of inflation, decided that economies were necessary in order to keep the company viable and, in 1974, pulled out of the North American market. Nevertheless production continued at an average 45-50,000 vehicles a year and, by 1976, one million Land Rovers had been produced. By April 1978, Land Rovers were coming out of the

Solihull factory at a rate of 1,250 units a week, and there were plans to increase this figure to 1,600 units within 12 months, with 2,700 vehicles a week planned for 1981.

Since the British Leyland takeover Rover had been part of BL's Specialist Cars Division, alongside Jaguar, Daimler and Triumph. This was fine for the car side of the business, but there was little synergy for the rather more specialised Land Rover vehicles. In July 1978, Leyland created two autonomous car-making operations - Austin-Morris Limited and Jaguar-Rover-Triumph Limited. Land-Rover became a separate unit within Jaguar-Rover-Triumph, eventually taking over all of the Solihull site, with Rover cars being produced elsewhere.

A month later it was announced that £280 million had been earmarked for development of the Land Rover range.

Some £30 million of this money had already been approved for Stage One, a V8-powered version of the 109in (2.77m) Series III.

Announced for export in February 1979, and making a show debut at Geneva that year, this was the first manifestation of the £280 million investment programme which eventually led to the development of the coil-sprung Defender. Stage One could be easily identified by the full-width black-painted front grille and redesigned bonnet, both necessary to accommodate the larger V8 engine.

Originally developed by General Motors' Buick Division in the US for leisure marine applications, this 3,528cc engine, which used many aluminium castings, allowed Land Rover to offer more power to customers with a minimum weight penalty. The engine was capable of considerable power output, going on to become a favourite with British hot-rodders, and was fitted in the military 101in (2.57m) forward control and the Defender, as well as in a range of high-performance low-volume sports cars. For the Stage One, the Land Rover's somewhat archaic brakes demanded

Above: Series III kitted out in desert patrol style. Note the roll-over bar, smoke launchers, front-mounted spare wheel and lack of doors, all features typical of the long-range patrol vehicle role established by David Stirling's SAS Jeeps. *(ST)*

that the engine was detuned to 95bhp, but it also produced excellent torque from low down in the revolutions range. It was coupled to the permanent four-wheel drive system of the Range Rover.

As far as is known no Stage Ones were supplied to the British armed forces although it is believed that the Royal Ulster Constabulary found the extra performance useful, particularly when combined with an armoured body. The Stage One also formed the basis for the half-tracked Laird Centaur (see page 152) and the Hotspur 6x6 armoured (page 171). It was also popular with the New Zealand Army and several Middle Eastern armies, including Iraq!

In April 1982, the 109in (2.77m) Series III chassis was offered with a new high-capacity pick-up body, to suit either a 2,205lb (1,000kg) or 2,866lb (1,300kg) payload, the latter featuring uprated suspension and shock absorbers. The pick-up bed was carried on a new type of subframe which projected 7in (18cm) beyond the rear cross-member. The vehicle could be supplied either with

a closed truck cab or with a full-length canvas hood. Engine options included both four and eight-cylinder units.

Production of the Series III, and the Stage One, continued until 1985 when both were replaced by what ought to have been called 'Stage Two', the coil-sprung Land Rover 90 and the 110… actually, this is not quite the whole story for 'Stage Two' also included the four-door Range Rover and, from around 1981, the use of new five-bearing engines across the entire product range.

But before the coil-sprung 90 and 110 models appeared, big changes were necessary at the Land Rover factory, with a new engine plant being built together with two extra production lines.

The military Series III

The development of the 88in (2.24m) 'lightweight' meant that very few short-wheelbase Series IIIs entered British Army service; almost all those that did were petrol-powered, although a small number of diesel-engined vehicles were supplied

to the Royal Navy and the Royal Air Force. A small number of 88in (2.24m) Series IIIs were also supplied in FFR (fitted for radio) guise, with 24V electrical systems.

Many of the 88in (2.24m) vehicles which were procured were in civilian guise, generally with the standard canvas top or with a hardtop, either the standard civilian unglazed top or a special military item with glazed side windows. Military-pattern vehicles could be identified by the special rear cross-member, rear towing hitch, military-type bumpers, lashing rings, and tie-down loops in the cargo area; twin 10 gal (45 litre) fuel tanks were placed under the front seats. There was provision for stowing a water jerrycan up against the rear bulkhead also rifle clips were fitted on the bulkhead; clips were provided on the rear tailgate for carrying the usual pioneer tools.

Optional equipment included a front-mounted 5,000lb (2,268kg) capacity mechanical drum winch, a 3,000lb (1,361kg) capacity capstan winch, and Aeon rubber helper springs.

Overseas customers were more enthusiastic, and short-wheelbase Series IIIs were procured in larger numbers by the Australian Army, these vehicles being recognisable by the square wheel-arch openings. Other customers included the Portuguese, Netherlands, New Zealand, Norwegian and South African Armies. A 24V equipped 4x2 version of the 88in (2.24m) Series III was developed for the Belgian Army, entering service in 1974. In 1978, the Danish Army was supplied with what was essentially a commercial Series III fitted with a 2,286cc diesel engine, and equipped with either a 12V or 24V electrical system.

As regards the 109in (2.77m) version, this could be considered the 'classic' military Land Rover, and the Ministry of Defence bought these, ultimately in very large numbers, from mid-1971 onwards.

Most were standard soft-top vehicles, differing from the civilian equivalent in only minor ways, although there were also standard military glazed and unglazed hardtops, the latter being preferred, but not exclusively, for FFR

Above: The so-called window hardtop was not a common sight on British military Land Rovers; this is a long-wheelbase Series III. *(PW)*

Above: By the time the Series III entered service, RAF vehicles were no longer painted blue but carried a yellow stripe around the green body; moutain rescue vehicles carried more distinctive markings. *(PW)*

vehicles. The RAF made particular use of the station wagons. The Royal Marines used a few truck-cab vehicles and there were also fire tenders constructed on an uprated version of the long-wheelbase Series III chassis.

Under the Carawagon name, R. J. Searle of Sunbury, Middlesex, produced a special commander's vehicle on the long-wheelbase Series III, which was employed by the British Army in small numbers as well as being exported. The rear body, which included an elevating roof, provided office accommodation large enough for three people to work and for two to sleep in overhead bunks. Cooking and air-conditioning facilities were also included.

Diesel engines were very much in the minority, with the four-cylinder 2,286cc petrol engine the standard fit. As with the 88in (2.27m) models, the military-type vehicles could be identified by the rear cross-member carrying a standard NATO-type towing hitch, military-pattern bumpers, the fitting of lashing rings, and tie-down loops in the rear compartment. Lighting equipment was often waterproofed and large numbers of vehicles were also supplied in FFR guise, with 24V electrical systems featuring a 90Ah alternator and full suppression facilities.

The most notable difference was inside the cab, where the centre seat was omitted to allow the installation of a military radio set. Like the 88in (2.27m) model, there were twin 10 gallon

(45 litre) fuel tanks fitted under the seats and rifle carrying clips were often fitted on the rear bulkhead. Although the dashboard would have been recognisable to any civilian Land Rover owner, there was an additional fascia-mounted lighting switch which controlled the use of a convoy lighting system, allowing the vehicle to operate under black-out conditions. Most of the interior trim to the cab was omitted.

In the rear body, longitudinal bench seats allowed the vehicle to carry eight fully-equipped soldiers.

A few truck cab and station wagon models also entered British military service.

Roles

The Series III appears to have been the most versatile of the military Land Rovers, being adapted for much the same range of roles as have already been described for the Series II, including aircraft crash-rescue, signals and communications, gun platform, helicopter starting vehicle, radar calibration unit, mine detector, MILAN launcher, TOW anti-tank missile launcher, 81mm mortar carrier, WOMBAT mount, carrier for missile computers and test equipment, utility and command vehicle, etc. It was also used as a towing vehicle for anti-aircraft missiles systems such as Tigercat and Rapier, and the British Army's Honourable Artillery Company was even seen

Technical specifications
Series III GS vehicles; 1971 to 1985
Typical nomenclature: truck, 3/4 ton, cargo, 4x4;
FV18071; Rover Series 3.

Engine: Land Rover; four cylinders; 2,286cc; petrol;
overhead valves; power output, 77bhp at 4,250rpm;
torque, 124 lbf/ft at 2,500rpm.
Transmission: 4F1Rx2; part-time 4x4.
Steering: recirculating ball, worm and nut.
Suspension: live axles on multi-leaf semi-elliptical
springs; hydraulic double-acting telescopic shock
absorbers; optional Aeon rubber helper springs.
Brakes: hydraulic; drums all-round; optional vacuum
servo-assistance.
Construction: welded box-section steel chassis;
steel-framed aluminium-panelled body.
Electrical system: 12V or 24V.

Dimensions
Length, (short wheelbase), 142in (3.61m);
(long wheelbase), 175in (4.45m).
Width, 64in (1.63m).
Height, (open vehicles, top in place), 78in (1.98m);
(closed vehicles), 81in (2.06m).
Wheelbase, 88in; 109in (2.24m; 2.77m).
Ground clearance, 8.5in (21.6cm).
Weight (short wheelbase), 2,900lb (1,315.44)
unladen, 4,453lb (2,020kg) laden;
long wheelbase 3,294lb (1,494.2kg) unladen,
5,905lb (2,678.5kg) laden.

Performance
Average speed, (road) 45mph (72.4kph);
(cross country) 10mph (16kph).
Range of action, 280 miles (450.6km).
Approach angle, 46°.
Departure angle, 30°.
Fording depth, 21in (53.3cm).

Stage One; 1979-85
Typical nomenclature: truck, 0.75 tonne, cargo, 4x4;
Land Rover 'Stage One'.

Engine: Land Rover; eight cylinders in 'V' configuration;
3,528cc; petrol; overhead valves; power output, 91bhp
at 3,500rpm; torque, 166 lbf/ft at 2,000rpm.
Transmission: 4F1Rx2; full-time 4x4; lockable centre
differential.
Steering: recirculating ball, worm and nut.

Suspension: live axles on multi-leaf semi-elliptical springs;
hydraulic double-acting telescopic shock absorbers.
Brakes: hydraulic; drums all-round; vacuum servo
assistance.
Construction: welded box-section steel chassis;
steel-framed aluminium-panelled body.
Electrical system: 12V or 24V.

Dimensions
Length, 177in (4.5m). Width, 66in (1.68m).
Height, (open vehicles, top fitted), 79in (2.0m);
(closed vehicles), 81in (2.06m).
Wheelbase, 109in (2.77m).
Ground clearance, 8.25in (21cm).
Weight, 3,828lb (1,736.4kg) unladen,
5,962lb (2,704.4kg) laden.

Performance
Maximum speed, (road) 80mph (129kph);
(cross country) 30mph (48kph).
Range of action, 250 miles (402.4km).
Approach angle, 46°;
Departure angle, 30°.
Fording depth, 21in (53.3cm).

FV numbers
- FV18061 Truck, 3/4 ton, cargo,
  4x4; Rover Series 3
- FV18062 Truck, 3/4 ton, cargo, FFR-24V, 4x4;
  Rover Series 3
- FV18063 Truck, 3/4 ton, gun radar calibration, 4x4;
  Rover Series 3
- FV18064 Truck, 3/4 ton, SAS, 4x4; Rover Series 3
- FV18065 Truck, 3/4 ton, ambulance, 2 stretcher, 4x4;
  Rover Series 3
- FV18066 Truck, 3/4 ton, ambulance, 2 stretcher,
  mountain rescue, 4x4; Rover Series 3
- FV18067 Truck, 3/4 ton, ambulance, 2/4 stretcher
  Mk 2, 4x4; Rover 9, 11, Rover Series 3
- FV18068 Truck, 3/4 ton, ambulance, 2/4 stretcher
  Mk 2, mountain rescue, 4x4; Rover Series 3
- FV18071 Truck, 3/4 ton, cargo, 4x4; Rover Series 3
- FV18072 Truck, 3/4 ton, cargo, FFR-24V, 4x4;
  Rover Series 3
- FV18073 Truck, 3/4 ton, ambulance, 2/4 stretcher
  Mk 2, 4x4; Rover Series 3
- FV18074 Truck, 3/4 ton, ambulance, 2/4 stretcher,
  mountain rescue, Mk 2, 4x4; Rover Series 3
- FV18081 Truck, 3/4 ton, cargo, 4x4, diesel;
  Rover Series 3

to use a 109in (2.77m) Series III for towing a ceremonial 25-pounder field gun.

In Northern Ireland, many vehicles were fitted with the Makrolon 'vehicle protection kit' (VPK) or 'Northern Ireland protection kit', which consisted of a hardtop, appliqué composite GRP and ballistic-protection panels to the doors, sills and bonnet, and an armoured shield for the windscreen. Twin doors were fitted at the rear, and a two-man hatch was installed in the roof. To deter would-be stone-throwers, wire-mesh screens were fitted over the windows and lights.

As with earlier vehicles, with the addition of a snorkel and the application of suitable water-proofing the vehicle could be made sufficiently amphibious to attempt a beach landing.

2.4 | 90, 110 and Defender

At the Geneva Motor Show in March 1983 Land Rover announced the new 'One Ten', the latest incarnation on the familiar long-wheelbase chassis. Whilst it cannot have been a complete surprise to the company's followers since the V8 petrol engine, permanent four-wheel drive transmission, and full-width grille had already been previewed in Stage One, it was nevertheless probably the most important vehicle produced by Land Rover since the announcement of the Series I in 1948.

The One Ten was the second tangible result of the £200 million investment programme which had first been manifest in Stage One. For some years Land Rover had been losing market to Toyota, whose Land Cruiser, whilst not popular in the UK, had been established as the world's best-selling 4x4. Companies such as Jeep and Nissan were equally keen to help themselves to Land Rover's market share elsewhere, and the One Ten was the company's response.

As regards technology, the One Ten was upgraded in every significant respect, taking advantage of developments which had made the Range Rover so successful.

Under the bonnet there was a choice of 2.25-litre petrol and diesel engines, as well as the 3.5-litre V8 petrol unit, which had already appeared in Stage One. The permanent four-wheel drive system of the Range Rover was employed, with its central lockable differential. The four-cylinder models were available with either a four or five-speed gearbox in combination with a new type of two-speed transfer box, whilst the V8 engine used the entire transmission system of the Range Rover, with the integral gearbox and transfer case. However, whilst the V8 may have offered sufficient power to customers who were happy to pay for petrol, the diesel engine remained less than satisfactory in what was becoming an increasingly heavy chassis. In Australia, the Land Rover diesel was felt to be seriously underpowered, even in the 2.5-litre form which was not to appear until 1985, and the 3,856cc Isuzu 4BD1 engine, which had been fitted in long-wheelbase Series IIs since 1982, continued to be offered in the One Ten.

Out went the leaf springs, and the chassis was completely redesigned to allow the use of long-travel, dual-rate coil springs. The live axles were located by means of radius arms, with a Panhard rod at the front and tubular trailing links at the rear, in combination with a centrally-mounted A frame. At extra cost, the rear axle could be fitted with the self-levelling rear suspension system as

used on the Range Rover, using a Boge Nivomat strut placed centrally above the axle. Optional power-assisted steering was available, and the system was redesigned to reduce the number of turns required, as well as to bring the turning circle down by 5ft (1.5m). Servo-assisted disc brakes were fitted to the front axle.

Although there was no significant body restyling, there was a new, and significantly larger, one-piece rubber-mounted flat wind-screen, full-width flush radiator grille with black-painted headlamp panels, and body-colour deformable plastic wheel-arch extensions. A range of new paint colours was offered and, for the first time, the body cappings were body-coloured giving the vehicle a rather more coherent appearance.

Inside, customers could specify air conditioning for the first time, and there were improved heating and ventilation facilities, also additional sound-proofing. The instrument panel was redesigned for ergonomic improvement.

Body options included a pick-up truck with either a full-length canvas top or steel cab, a high-capacity pick-up with a wider, longer rear body, full-length hardtop and station wagon. A so-named County station wagon was also offered, this vehicle had the self-levelling rear axle and power-assisted steering fitted as standard. For the

Top: A Military Police Land Rover passing a Challenger tank in Bosnia. *(Crown Copyright)*
Above: The first One Ten in March 1983. *(TM)*

Above: Defender 110 station wagon with an unusual roll cage, roof hatch and weapons mount. *(TM)*

first time, the station wagon lacked what was known as the 'safari' double-skin roof.

The One Ten went on sale in 1983, although it does not appear to have fully replaced the 109in (2.77m) Series III until 1985. In the summer of that year, the range was further extended by the inclusion of a 6x6 chassis and a stretched 4x4 with a 127in (3.23m) wheelbase.

The V8-powered 6x6 had been developed by SMC using Range Rover axles in a variation of the drive-line used by Sandringham on their Sandringham Six, the major difference being that the rear-most axle could be de-selected. The 127in (3.23m) chassis was initially described as the One Two Seven, and was offered with a six-seater crew cab and a shortened version of the high-capacity pick-up bed.

Obviously it was just a matter of time before the short-wheelbase Series III was given the same treatment, and the Ninety, as it was now called, appeared in June 1984. Development work on

the short-wheelbase version had actually started in 1978, but it had been held back in favour of the longer-wheelbase One Ten.

As yet, there was no V8 engine option for the Ninety and, in this case, the engine choice was either the 2.25-litre four-cylinder petrol engine or a 2.5-litre four-cylinder diesel which was effectively a longer-stroke version of the old 2.25-litre unit. The new diesel engine had been introduced in February of that year, when it had replaced the old 2.25-litre unit as fitted in the One Ten. Both engines were mated to a five-speed gearbox. Despite the name, the wheelbase actually measured up at 92.9in (2.36m), and the vehicle was some 4in (10cm) longer than the 88in (2.24m) Series III which it replaced, yet had less rear overhang.

Like the One Ten, the Ninety was available in a full range of body styles, including canvas or steel-cabbed pick-up truck, full-length hardtop and station wagon. The County version was

equipped with a range of up-market fitments including carpets!

All of the improvements which had been made in the One Ten were reflected in the Ninety and, at the time of the Ninety's launch, Land Rover also took the opportunity to make some interior improvements to the One Ten, including, for the first time, wind-up windows… although sliding glass was still fitted to the rear-most side windows of the station wagons.

The other big news of 1984 was that, once again, the Land Rover company changed hands, now becoming part of the British Aerospace Group (BAe).

With both models in the market, Land Rover could begin to assess their impact on sales and, whilst the new models had been extremely well received, it was not enough to reverse the sales decline that had started in 1982. Sales during 1984 and 1985 were lower than at any time since the late 1950s; the annual average sale of 33,500 vehicles for each of these two years compares to figures which had previously been closer to 45,000 or even 50,000.

More changes were afoot when, in May 1985, the V8 engine was also offered for the Ninety in combination with the five-speed gearbox. The vehicle was assembled at the Santana factory in Spain. This made the Ninety into an excellent high-performance off-roader, more than capable of competing on equal terms with Japanese-manufactured vehicles. In August, the standard four-cylinder petrol engine was upgraded to 2,495cc and the old Series III finally went out of production. In October 1986 the diesel was given an optional turbo-charger, which uplifted the power output by 25%; this proved a popular modification and it was not long before the turbo diesel became the norm.

Minor trim modifications were made inside the cab and, outside, the external bonnet lock was finally removed in favour of a remote cable release.

Above: The Defender can be recognised by its one-piece windscreen, flush-fronted grille and distinctive rubber wheel-arch eyebrows. This is the standard 110in GS vehicle with a hardtop. *(ST)*

Top: Defender 110 with the doors and windscreen removed. *(PW)*

Above: Extended wheelbase Defender 130 with a communications shelter; when fitted with a different body, these Defender 130s were commonly used by the RAF for towing Rapier missile batteries. *(ST)*

But sadly, none of this was enough to improve sales. In 1986, total sales were down again, at just 22,026 and the following year, the total number of vehicles sold was the lowest since 1953 to 1954, at just 20,475.

In 1990, the range was rebranded as Defender. Although the Ninety and One Ten names were retained, the One Two Seven was mysteriously changed to One Thirty.

At the same time, a new 2.5-litre turbo-charged inter-cooled diesel engine was introduced across all three model variants. Civilian customers had a choice of four engines for the Defender Ninety and One Ten; 2.5-litre four-cylinder and 3.5-litre V8 petrol engines, and 2.5-litre diesel engines available in naturally-aspirated or turbo-charged form; the Defender One Thirty was available only with the V8 petrol engine or the turbo-charged diesel. All three models were offered with a five-speed gearbox, albeit that the type fitted to the V8-engined vehicles was of a different design. There was also a two-speed transfer case and the permanent four-wheel-drive system which had originally been designed for the Range Rover, with a lockable centre differential.

Body options remained unchanged, with a canvas or steel-cabbed pick-up truck, full-length hardtop, and station wagon; the crew cab also remained available on the One Thirty and was eventually also made available on the One Ten.

More changes came in 1993, when the 200 Tdi diesel engine was superseded by the more powerful 300 Tdi and, in 1995, the five-cylinder TD5 turbo-diesel was introduced.

There have been two additional changes of ownership since the British Aerospace take-over in 1984. The Rover Group was sold to BMW in 1994, with Land Rover hived off and sold to Ford in the year 2000, at the same time as the ill-fated Phoenix Group took over the Rover car businesses.

The military Defender

In the same way that the British Army purchased the Series II when the Series I went out of production and then moved to the Series III when the Series II was no longer available, so it was natural that purchases made after the introduction of the Ninety and One Ten would specify the new models.

Similarly, overseas customers started purchasing the new models as soon as the Series III went out of production. Although some military users, notably the Irish Defence Force and occasionally the RAF, preferred to buy civilian machines, special military demonstrators for the One Ten were developed during 1983. A Middle Eastern customer, who ordered 900 vehicles in June 1984, made the first significant purchases, and production of the military One Ten began in 1985. Special military variants of the One Ten were also built by Otakar in Turkey, and by JRA in Sydney for the Australian Army from 1987, the latter being powered by Isuzu diesel engines.

Military versions of the Ninety appeared in 1986 but, in both cases, Land Rover continued to lose ground to Mercedes-Benz whose Steyr-built 'G-Wagen' was becoming increasingly popular with various European armies.

Land Rover hit back by marketing the new Ninety and One Ten vehicles directly at the defence sectors. Although special military brochures had been designed for the 'lightweight' and the '101', for the first time, the company produced dedicated sales material for the standard vehicles, intended to appeal to military procurement personnel. It is interesting to note that the military customer was not expected to cope with the trendy 'Ninety' or 'One Ten' names, and the vehicles were referred to simply as the '90' and the '110' and then, after the

Top: A pair of long-wheelbase hardtop vehicles, one fitted for radio (FFR), the other used by REME as part of a recovery team. *(PW)*

Above: The Defender chassis also lent itself to development as a special operations vehicle. *(BM)*

Defender name was adopted in 1990, as the Defender 90 and Defender 110.

Soon after the introduction of the Defender name, Land Rover started to refer to the military offering as the 'core military Defender', presenting the range as a family of related vehicles with a range of options from which customers could choose to effectively customise vehicles to suit the anticipated role. Much was made of the commonality of parts across the range and the logistic benefits which this could bring, as well as the reduced need for the training of driving and maintenance staff.

In theory, military customers could choose from the same range of engine options as the civilians but, in practice, few vehicles were sold with the 2.25-litre petrol engine, most customers opting for the V8 petrol engine or the 2.25-litre diesel. When the new turbo-diesel 250 Tdi engine was introduced in 1986, this was also added to the military line-up and, although it proved a popular option overseas, none was specified for British Army service… even though the British Army had begun the switch to diesel-powered Land Rovers at

around this time. The Irish Defence Force was less conservative and when the 250 Tdi appeared, a number of existing petrol-engined 110s were converted to diesel power in the IDF's own workshops using kits supplied from Solihull, but the conversion was unsuccessful largely because the original gearboxes were retained, with the ratios proving unsuitable for the slower-revving diesels.

Available body styles were listed in the brochures, including hardtop, soft-top, station wagon, and pick-up; stripped-down patrol (DPV) and special operations vehicles (SOV) were also available. The list of variants for the 110 also included an armoured body using a composite glass-fibre/phenolic armour material manufactured by Courtaulds, and the 130 was also offered with a crew cab, ambulance or box body, and was equally capable of accommodating shelter bodies such as might be required for electronics repair, field kitchen or mobile workshop roles. The 110 and 130 were also available in chassis-cab form and Land Rover prepared a special demonstrator vehicle mounting a 106mm recoilless anti-tank

gun on the 110in (2.79m) chassis as a replacement for the similar vehicle on the discontinued 'lightweight' platform.

An FFR (fitted for radio) option was available for the hardtop and soft-top versions of the 110 which consisted of two 12V 100Ah batteries, radio table, two radio operators' seats, antenna mountings on front wings and rear body, radio power terminal with ammeter, and a hand throttle to enable the engine to recharge the batteries whilst the vehicle was stationary.

Optional equipment, generally available across the range, included auxiliary fuel tanks, black-out lighting, infra-red reflective paint, towing equipment, air-conditioning, slings for helicopter-lifting, stowage for pioneer tools on the bonnet, lashing cleats in the rear body, jerrycan stowage lockers, side-hinged tailgate, choice of bonnet or tailgate spare wheel mounts, and towing equipment. All models were available with a choice of 12V or 24V electrical systems, using a commercial 65Ah or 120Ah 12V alternator, or suppressed single or twin 50Ah 24V alternator. There was also a

range of tyre options available to suit different terrains, and once the Defender XD had been launched, the same heavy-duty wheel was also offered on the standard military Defender.

The payload range was said to cover 1,655lb (751kg) all the way up to 5,510lb (2,499kg), and the 110 was also available with heavy-duty suspension which upped the gross vehicle weight to 7,7160lb (3500kg).

Roles

The 90 was known by the British Army as 'truck, utility, light' (TUL), while its bigger brother, the 110 was described as 'truck, utility, medium' (TUM). The 130 was sometimes referred to as 'truck, utility, medium, heavy duty' (TUM-HD). These descriptions were not unique to the Defender. The Pinzgauer, which had started to replace the Land Rover in certain roles, was similarly named.

Following in the footsteps of the Series III, the Defender lends itself for adaptation to every conceivable military role, including general service, military police, signals and

Above: British Army Land Rover loaded with troops and kit during the first Gulf War, 1990-91. The vehicle is equipped with radios and a General Purpose machine gun (GPMG). *(IWM)*

Above: Defender 110 desert patrol vehicle. *(ST)*

communications vehicle, gun platform, helicopter starting vehicle, mortar carrier, mine detector, anti-tank missile launcher, electronics shelter, radio direction finders, utility and command vehicle, etc. In various roles, the top, windscreen or doors were often omitted to lower the vehicle's profile and, of course, there are also dedicated special operations vehicles available.

Although it is most generally encountered in ambulance form, the 130 also lends itself to use as a communications and repair vehicle or as an artillery tractor; the RAF Regiment employ special-bodied 130s to tow Rapier missile batteries and to carry support equipment, having selected it in competition against the Italian-manufactured Iveco 40-10WM.

As with earlier vehicles, with the addition of a snorkel and the application of suitable waterproofing, the vehicle could be made sufficiently amphibious to drive through the surf from a landing craft.

Right: Defender 110 special operations vehicle was originally designed for the US Rangers. *(ST)*

Technical specifications
Defender 90 and 110; 1983 on
Nomenclature: truck, utility, light (TUL), 4x4; truck, utility, medium (TUM), 4x4; Land Rover Defender 90, 110.

Engine: Land Rover 300 Tdi; four cylinders; 2,506cc; overhead valves; direct-injection turbo-charged diesel; power output, 111bhp at 4,000rpm; torque, 195 lbf/ft at 1,800rpm. Other engine options available including 2.5 litre and 3.5 litre petrol, and 2.5 litre diesel.
Transmission: 5F1Rx2; full-time 4x4; centre lockable differential.
Steering: worm and roller; optional power assistance.
Suspension: live axles on long-travel, dual-rate coil springs; axle location by Panhard rod at the front, and 'A' frame at the rear; hydraulic double-acting telescopic shock absorbers.
Brakes: dual servo-assisted hydraulic; discs all-round.
Construction: reinforced welded box-section steel chassis; steel-framed aluminium-panelled body.
Electrical system: 12V or 24V.

Dimensions
Length, (short wheelbase) 153in (3.9m), (long wheelbase) 175in (4.45m).
Width, 70in (1.78m).
Height, 80in (2.03m) unladen.
Wheelbase, 90in; 110in (2.3m; 2.8m).
Ground clearance, 7.5in; 8.5in (19cm; 21.6cm).
Weight (short wheelbase), 3,729lb (1,691.5kg) unladen, 4,125lb (1,871kg) laden; (long wheelbase) 4,717lb (2,139.6kg) unladen, 6,710lb (3,043.7kg) laden.

Performance
Maximum speed, (road) 75mph (120.7kph); (cross country) 35mph (56kph).
Range of action, 145-165 miles (233-266km).
Approach angle, 48° (short wheelbase), 50° (long wheelbase);

Departure angle, 49° (short wheelbase models), 35° (long wheelbase models).
Fording depth: 20in.

Defender 130; 1984 on
Nomenclature: truck, utility, medium, heavy-duty (TUM-HD), 4x4; Land Rover Defender 130.

Engine: Land Rover 300 Tdi; four cylinders; 2,506cc; overhead valves; direct-injection turbo-charged diesel; power output, 111bhp at 4,000rpm; torque, 195 lbf/ft at 1,800rpm. Other engine options available including 2.5 litre and 3.5 litre petrol, and 2.5 litre diesel.
Transmission: 5F1Rx2; full-time 4x4; centre lockable differential.
Steering: worm and roller; optional power assistance.
Suspension: live axles on long-travel, dual-rate coil springs; axle location by Panhard rod at the front, and 'A' frame at the rear; hydraulic double-acting telescopic shock absorbers; co-axial helper springs at rear.
Brakes: dual servo-assisted hydraulic; discs all-round.
Construction: reinforced welded box-section steel chassis; steel-framed aluminium-panelled body.
Electrical system: 12V or 24V.

Dimensions
Length, 202in (5.13m).
Width, 70in (1.78m). Height, 80in (2.03m) unladen.
Wheelbase, 127in (3.23m).
Ground clearance, 8.5in (21.6cm).
Weight, 4,589lb (2,081.6kg) unladen, 7,700lb (3,492.7kg) laden.

Performance
Maximum speed, (road) 75mph (120.7kph); (cross country) 30mph (56kph).
Range of action, 145 miles (233km).
Approach angle, 50°;
Departure angle, 35°.
Fording depth, 20in (50.8cm).

Below: Two long-wheelbase Defender hardtop FFR vehicles in service with the British Army. *(BM)*

2.5 | Wolf Defender XD

Although the Defender range remains an important part of the Land Rover military offering, at least two military customers have also purchased the Defender 'XD' - or 'extra duty' - a purpose-designed military Land Rover which was developed to meet the requirements of the British Ministry of Defence (MoD).

By the middle to late 1980s, the British Army's Land Rover fleet consisted of a miscellany of elderly petrol-engined Series IIIs, large numbers of diesel Series IIIs, and early 90 and 110 Defenders. The 'lightweights' and forward-control 101 gun tractors also remained in service but were unlikely to be replaced on a like-for-like basis. However, the MoD was keen to replace all of these vehicles with a common design which would be able to accommodate all of the roles covered by the existing vehicles as well as offering enhanced performance and increased reliability.

In 1988, a specification was prepared for what was being described at the time as the 'truck, utility, light, high specification' (TUL-HS), and 'truck, utility, medium, high specification' (TUM-HS), to replace the standard long- and short-wheelbase vehicles. There was no longer any requirement for the 'lightweight', but a specification was also drawn-up for a so-called 'TUH' (truck, utility, heavy - later to become TUM-HD or 'heavy duty')

to replace the forward-control 101 in the gun tractor role, and to provide a 130in (3.30m) wheelbase battlefield ambulance.

The specification, for what later became known as the Wolf Defender XD, described the required operating parameters, calling for considerable improvements in performance compared with the, then current Defender. The MoD classified the vehicle as one which would provide 'improved medium mobility', which meant that it was required to offer the following minimum performance:

- maximum under-vehicle angle, 155°
- mean maximum ground pressure, 350kPa
- minimum approach and departure angles, front 40°, rear 38°
- minimum turning circle, 39.4ft (12m)
- static stability on side-slope, maximum 33°
- towing capability, 7,716lb (3,500kg) using over-run brakes on the trailer; 8,818lb (4,000kg) with power brakes
- unprepared fording depth, 23.6in (60cm)

Even though Land Rover supplied prototypes for all three of the specified vehicle types, the contract was considered to be an open competition and, despite Land Rover's impressive record of supplying the British Army, their involvement was not a foregone conclusion. However, it is interesting to note that this was the first time that Land Rover had been involved in developing an entirely-military variant of the standard short- and long-wheelbase vehicles.

The MoD contacted 19 manufacturers across the globe to gauge interest in the TUL/TUM/TUH project in the hope that the Defence Evaluation & Research Agency (DERA) would be able to assess the performance of as wide a selection of vehicles as possible. As it happened, the 'invitation to tender', which was issued in March 1991, went to just three companies - Land Rover, Iveco, and Pinzauer.

There were two contracts on offer. The first covered 8,000 tactical utility vehicles in the 'light' and 'medium' classes, in other words

TUL and TUM, whilst the second, which was put out for bids a year later, called for 800 battlefield ambulances. It was also planned that the TUM-HD vehicle would replace the 101 and the unreliable Reynolds Boughton RB44; this contract was eventually awarded to Pinzgauer following competition with a

Above: Early Wolf prototype vehicles had a rear-mounted spare wheel and a distinctive bonnet bulge. This is the long-wheelbase TUM variant. *(PW)*

Right: 16 Air Assault Brigade during an Aviation Battle Group Excercise at West Freugh airfield. The Brigade are the British Army's rapid reaction specialists, and can be deployed anywhere in the world at 48 hours notice. *(Mark Owens/Crown Copyright)*

modified wide-bodied version of Land Rover's TUM which proved unsatisfactory.

In November 1991 the MoD issued a contract to Land Rover for the construction of 'evaluation trials' vehicles. At the same time, it was announced that DERA had taken the decision to eliminate Iveco and Pinzgauer from the first trials programme without even assessing their vehicles, so Land Rover entered these initial trials alone.

The same three manufacturers - Iveco, Land Rover and Pinzgauer - were also asked to supply vehicles for the ambulance programme.

Development

Paul Markwick was appointed to lead Land Rover's 45-strong project team and there followed an intensive 18-month programme under the project name 'Wolf', and later known as 'Wolf 1', to upgrade the so-called 'core military Defender' in an effort to meet the specification.

Dating from 1984, the core military Defender was not much more than a development of the Defender 90 and 110 models, both of which could trace their lineage right back to the Series I of 1948. In an effort to update the vehicle's performance,

the team fitted the turbo-charged diesel engine derived from the civilian 'Gemini 2' project - a kind-of halfway house between the 200Tdi and the later 300Tdi. The engine breathed through distinctive dust-extractor air intakes behind the front wheel arches. A heavy-duty clutch and gearbox were fitted, together with an oil cooler, permanent four-wheel drive and a lockable centre differential. There were servo-assisted disc brakes all-round, and power-assisted steering, and the vehicle included large numbers of relatively-

Above: By the time the vehicle was accepted for service, the spare wheel had moved to the side and the bonnet bulge had disappeared; this is the TUL variant.
Below: Land Rover also built a contender for the TUH variant but it did not progress beyond prototype stage. *(PW [both])*

Right: This vehicle carries the distinctive composite hardtop and is clearly fitted for radio (FFR); note the hose carried on the bonnet - this is used to duct exhaust fumes away from the vehicle during whilst the radio is in operation and the vehicle is stationary. *(PW)*

Below: Snorkel air intake for wading operations. *(PW)*

minor changes to improve reliability and reduce maintenance requirements.

The first prototypes were delivered in May 1993, with examples of the 90in (2.3m) wheelbase TUL, the 110in (2.8m) TUM, and the wide-bodied 130in (3.3m) TUM-HD.

It was obvious that this was no ordinary Defender. At the rear, a side-mounted tailgate carried the spare wheel, and the TUM variant was fitted with a front-mounted winch. The bonnet of FFR (fitted for radio) variants had a prominent power bulge to accommodate a 24V alternator and its drive belts. The vehicle had a wide track and a purposeful, nose-down stance which distinguished it from the civilian Defenders.

However, within a few months, it was clear that Land Rover's engineers had not gone far enough.

With hindsight, it should perhaps have been clear that a 'warmed over' Defender would not be sufficient to meet the specification. The trials

highlighted weaknesses in a number of areas, including the transmission, axle casings, half-shafts, differentials, steering gear, and suspension. Both the chassis and body were also found to be lacking structural integrity and there were problems with engine overheating, and overheating of the gearbox.

The trials were stopped in September 1993.

Markwick and his team were given the opportunity to reconsider their design and prepare new prototypes for a second round of trials. One year was set aside for the re-development work and Land Rover was obliged to submit a redesigned vehicle within this period if the company wished to remain in contention. There was insufficient time to develop a completely-new vehicle, but there was no opportunity to pitch again should the second round of prototypes fail. Unable to go back to the drawing board, the team carefully

addressed every criticism and failure of the vehicles, beefing up or changing components, introducing changes, and making significant improvements in virtually all areas.

The new prototypes for the 90in (2.3m) and 110in (2.8m) vehicles, now identified as 'Wolf 2', were delivered to the MoD in September 1994… by which time Land Rover had been taken over by BMW. The 130in (3.3m) TUM(HD) variant was abandoned.

Wolf 2 was considerably more successful than its predecessor and, this time there were few problems. After a trials period covering more than eight months and 55,000 miles (88,511.5km), the vehicles were said to have achieved the stated reliability requirement. The short-wheelbase TUL-HS achieved a final 'mean distance between failure' (MDBF) figure of 11,679 miles (18,795km), whilst the TUM-HS, clocked up 4,250 miles (6,839.5km); in each case, this was

Above: With the windscreen and windows well protected by mesh, this TUM variant was photographed in Iraq. *(PW)*

Above: A Wolf TUM variant struggling through the Iraq mud. *(PW)*

Below: Some vehicles serving in Iraq have been seen to have a small air-conditioning unit installed in the locker ahead of the rear wheel which is normally used for jerrycans. *(PW)*

measured against a requirement of 2,325 miles (3,741.6km) on a typical simulated battlefield mission.

The final choice of engine was the 'Gemini 3', perhaps better known as the 300 Tdi, a 2,495cc direct-injection turbo-charged diesel unit producing 111bhp at 4,000rpm. Power was conveyed to all four wheels through a diaphragm clutch and then via a five-speed gearbox and two-speed transfer case, which incorporated a third, lockable differential.

Chassis cross-members were strengthened, and the front bulkhead, cab top rails and sills were reinforced; there was a new radiator-surround frame. The rear load bed was also strengthened and reinforced, to provide a 20% increase in payload.

The live axles were suspended on the same long-travel coil springs as found on the Defender, with Panhard rod and radius arm location and telescopic dual-action shock absorbers. The springs and dampers were both uprated. A Rover axle was used at the front, and a Salisbury unit at the rear but, in both cases, the differential housings were increased in thickness to 0.25in (6mm), and four-pinion differential gears were used, along with strengthened half-shafts. Recirculating-ball power steering was fitted as standard, with heavy-duty protection for the normally-exposed parts of the steering gear.

Dual-circuit servo-assisted disc brakes were fitted all round. Even the wheels were new, with a heavy-duty 16in rim developed especially for the Wolf by GKN; tyres were 7.50x16 Goodyear G90, with Michelin XZL available as an option.

Externally, the spare wheel was moved to a high positioned side mount and the distinctive FFR power bulge was removed. The distinctive triangular air intakes on the front wings were retained, providing a useful recognition point, as were the plastic wheel-arch extenders of the original Defender. Both soft-top and hardtop variants were produced, the latter fitted with unique self-coloured plastic hardtops with a vision hatch in the cab roof.

For the crew, the TUL provides accommodation for two men in the front and four in the rear, while the TUM will accommodate eight men and includes a stowage compartment ahead of the rear wheels for jerrycans; on vehicles recently used in Iraq, this compartment appears to have been used as a housing for an air-conditioning unit. A full roll cage was fitted, together with front seat belts and anchorage points for rear belts.

All TUL/TUM vehicles are fitted with a 24V electrical system using a high-output alternator, and approximately half the fleet is fitted for radio. There were no other variants at the time of launch, but the Wolf can also be equipped with the so-called 'weapons mount installation kit' (WMIK), which allows the vehicle to carry either two 7.62mm general-purpose machine guns (GMPG - 'gimpies'), or a GPMG and a .50 calibre Browning. An armoured variant, known as 'Snatch' has recently started to appear in Iraq, a number having been issued to the Iraqi security forces.

Production XD

In 1995, the production Wolf Defender XD was unveiled to the public at the Royal Navy and British Army Equipment Exhibition. In February 1996, the MoD awarded Land Rover a production contract for almost 8,000 vehicles worth some £200 million. Production was started later that year.

During the first 12 months of production, between September 1996 and September 1997, vehicles were randomly selected from the production line for what were known as 'production confirmatory trials'.

The Defender XD started to enter service on 1 April 1997, with the vehicles having a planned service life of around 15 years - which means that they are likely to remain in service until around 2012. By October 1998 nearly 8,000 vehicles had been constructed, and by the end of the century the XD had replaced virtually all of the British Army's original Series III vehicles.

Uniquely, the vehicles were supplied to the MoD with a five-year, or 46,604 miles (75,000km), parts and labour warranty which included three years' cover on batteries, and one year on tyres and exhausts. Land Rover's worldwide dealership network means that the warranty is available more-or-less anywhere that British troops are deployed, and this arrangement has worked successfully in Germany, Italy, the former Yugoslavia, Cyprus, Egypt, Israel and Albania. The warranty also makes provision for trained unit personnel to do the work under operational circumstances, using Land Rover-supplied parts. Finally, the MoD has also secured a one-year 'Land Rover assist' package, similar to that offered to civilian customers, which is valid in the UK and Germany... but, sadly, not in Iraq or Afghanistan!

The total British Army production figure was 7,925, broken down as 1,411 short-wheelbase vehicles (TUL), and 6,514 of the long-wheelbase TUM variant. At one time, apparently, serious consideration was given to abandoning the TUL variant altogether, and it only survived because of its use by, for example, 16 Air Assault Brigade.

Production terminated in October 1998 and there have been no repeat orders in the UK.

Below: Left-hand drive hardtop Wolf TUM, possibly ex-Dutch Forces. *(ST)*

Above: A pair of Wolf TUM hardtop variants on patrol in Iraq. *(PW)*

Right: Wolf TUL variant driving up a landing craft ramp. With the addition of a snorkel and the application of suitable waterproofing, all Wolf variants could be made sufficiently amphibious to drive through the surf from a landing craft. *(PW)*

In service, the Defender XD has proved to be a fast, reliable and extremely capable machine. The second Iraq War and in Afghanistan the vehicle is used over the most extreme terrain without difficulty.

As well as serving with the British Army, the Defender XD also entered service with the Dutch Marines, with some 71 TUM variants being ordered in 1997 to replace a similar number of 110s. The XD was selected, at least partly, because it was the only European vehicle of this type which could meet the Dutch waterproofing specification.

Above: Wolf TUM variant with the British Army weapons mount installation kit (WMIK) which allows weapons to be mounted on the roll cage. Paratroopers from the 3rd Battalion, Parachute Regiment, train using their heavily armed vehicle and a Westland Lynx of 3 Regiment Army Air Corps. Both units form the backbone of 16 Air Assault Brigade. (*Chris Fletcher/Crown Copyright*)

Technical specification
Defender Wolf XD-90 and XD-110; 1996 on
Nomenclature: truck, utility, light (TUL), 4x4; truck, utility, medium (TUM), 4x4; Land Rover Defender XD-90, XD-110.

Engine: Land Rover 300 Tdi; four cylinders; 2,506cc; overhead valves; direct-injection turbo-charged diesel; power output, 111bhp at 4,000rpm; torque, 195 lbf/ft at 1,800rpm.
Transmission: 5F1Rx2; full-time 4x4; centre lockable differential.
Steering: power-assisted worm and roller.
Suspension: reinforced live axles on long-travel coil springs; axle location by Panhard rod at the front, and 'A' frame at the rear; hydraulic double-acting telescopic shock absorbers.
Brakes: dual servo-assisted hydraulic; discs all-round.
Construction: reinforced welded box-section steel chassis; steel-framed aluminium-panelled body.
Electrical system: 12V or 24V.

Dimensions
Length, (short wheelbase) 151in (3.84m), (long wheelbase) 179in (4.55m).
Width, 70in (1.8m).
Height, 80in (2.03m) unladen.
Wheelbase, 90in; 127in (2.3m; 3.23m).
Ground clearance, 9.5in (24cm).
Weight, (short wheelbase) 4,400lb (1,996kg) unladen, 5,720lb (2,594.6kg) laden; (long wheelbase) 4,717lb (2,139.6kg) unladen, 7,357lb (3,337kg) laden.

Performance
Maximum speed, (road) 80mph (129kph); (cross country) 35mph (56kph).
Range of action, 360 miles (580km).
Approach angle, 51°.
Departure angle, 52° (short wheelbase models), 35° (long wheelbase models).
Fording depth: 24in (61cm); 60in (1.5m) with snorkel.

2.6 | ½-ton Lightweight

At the time of its introduction the so-called 'lightweight' was the closest thing to a purpose-designed military Land Rover. As regards its unladen weight, it was something in the order of 150lb (68kg) heavier than the 88in (2.24m) Series IIA Rover 8 from which it was derived. But, in stripped down form, it could be reduced to around 2,660lb (1,206.6kg) compared to 3,220lb (1,460.6kg) for the standard cargo vehicle… hence the name.

The notion of producing an air-portable vehicle capable of carrying a useful military payload, and towing a support weapon, dated from the latter stages of World War Two, when military strategists started advocating the fast deployment of troops and equipment by glider or parachute. Early experiments concentrated on specialised lightweight vehicles, which differed considerably from their standard production equivalents.

During the 1950s the British Army trialed the Steyr Haflinger and the Austin Mini-Moke, as well as experimental vehicles such as the Triumph Pony and the Austin Ant, for the air-portable role. The Royal Marines carried Citroën 2CV pick-ups on the carriers HMS *Bulwark* and HMS *Albion*, flying them ashore slung under Wessex helicopters.

However, what the Army and the Royal Marines really needed was a standard utility vehicle, such as a Land Rover, which could be easily delivered by air… but, with an unladen weight of 3,146lb (1,427kg), even the 88in (2.24m) Series IIA was too heavy. The Ministry of Defence had

actually gone on record as stating that 'the current WD short wheelbase Land Rover is too wide and too heavy (…for certain air-portable roles)'. Nevertheless, thousands were in service and, reluctant to abandon the obvious benefits of standardisation, the Ministry was clearly not keen to buy a completely different vehicle for the air-portable role.

An 88in (2.24m) Series II had already been cut down to the minimum for the Royal Marines in the Land Rover experimental shop and was spotted in the workshop by some senior Ministry of Defence officials. This, they decided, was just what was needed and, in 1964, an official specification was issued describing a 'lightweight version of the short-wheelbase Land Rover'. It was intended to be carried by RAF heavy air-lift aircraft, including Argosy, Beverley, and could also be underslung beneath the Westland Wessex HC2 helicopter.

The specification called for a maximum overall width of 60in (1.5m), which would allow two

vehicles to be carried in the width of an Argosy fuselage; the unladen weight was not to exceed 2,500lb (1,134kg) for the 12V cargo variant, or 3,100lb (1,406kg) for the FFR (fitted for radio), and it was to be capable of carrying a 1,000lb (453.6kg) payload, including driver, with a range of 300 miles (483km). It was to be fitted with lifting points, and be able to tow a 10cwt (508kg) trailer.

This was all very well in principle but, for the short-wheelbase Rover 8 to be capable of fulfilling the 'lightweight' role as defined, it would have to shed in the order of 500lb (226.8kg). However, the War Office declared that, in order to simplify parts stockholding, the engine, gearbox, axles, suspension, and steering were to be identical to the standard vehicle which meant that all of the weight saving would have to be made in the bodywork.

Design

In conjunction with the Chertsey-based Fighting Vehicles Research & Development Establishment

Above: Standard 'Rover 1' (Series IIA derived) 'lightweight' from the second contract which called for 1,000 vehicles with an in-service date of 1969. *(PW)*

Left: The first prototype, which appeared in 1965, had this distinctive frontal appearance. *(TM)*

(FVRDE) - and subsequently, with their successors, the Military Vehicles and Engineering Establishment (MVEE) - Rover's design team rose to the challenge. Tom Barton assigned the role of

Top: The doors, windscreen, side panels, tailgate, tilt and bumpers could quickly be removed to reduce the total weight of the vehicle. *(TM)*

Above: Although this Series 3 'lightweight' is in private hands, hardtops were designed for the British Army from about 1969. *(PR)*

project engineer to Mike Broadhead, who was assisted by Norman Busby. By the time the vehicle was ready for production, both Broadhead and Busby were busy on other projects and Bob Seager became the project engineer.

In 1965, the first prototype of what was being called the 'general service lightweight' appeared. It was handed over to FVRDE for testing later that same year. The 'lightweight' was based on the standard Rover 8 short-wheelbase chassis, using the FV18032 for the cargo or GS variant, and the FV18031 for the FFR. The chassis itself was modified by the addition of a brace across the

main members at the front; the front bumper was narrower and could be removed, and the additional chassis bracing was intended to reduce flexing when the vehicle was used in this condition. The gearbox cross-member was also easily removed.

In assembled form, the 'lightweight' appeared to have little in common with its 'heavier' relatives. Although unmistakably a Land Rover, it had that angular, rather ill-fitting appearance which often passes for 'combat chic' in purpose-designed military vehicles.

Visually, the 'lightweight' had a more Jeep-like appearance than the Series IIA from which it had been derived. In part this was due to the open, flat-topped front mudguards - which Rover rather mystifyingly described as improving 'accessibility and ease of cleaning of the wheels and wheel arches', and the huge angular rear wheel arches. But the bonnet, too, was noticeably deeper, narrower and more angular than the standard item. The radiator was protected by a typical wire-mesh Land Rover-style grille more akin to that which had been used on the Series I. A bottom-hinged folding tailgate was fitted at the rear.

Under the bonnet, the prototype was powered by the standard 2,286cc petrol engine, with the oil cooler omitted to save weight. Similarly, the gearbox and steering components

of the Rover 8 were also used. The heavy-duty military-type suspension was removed in favour of the standard civilian-pattern springs. Whilst the axles were generally identical to the production items, the track was narrower - which meant that shorter half-shafts were used - and the drive flanges were redesigned to the reduced overall width.

The designers had reduced the overall width, in stripped form, by 4in (10cm) to a total of 60in (1.5m) - which meant that the bulkhead was all-new. Weight-saving features included the use of 6.00x16 tyres, rather than the standard 6.50x16, mounted on one-piece commercial-type rims… although the standard wheels and tyres could, apparently, fit in the wheel arches if required. The designers must have been desperate to save weight since webbing straps were used to secure the spare wheel on the bonnet, the rubbing strips in the cargo area were omitted, and there was no wire-mesh fly screen in the scuttle vent.

The 'lightweight' offered no particular advantages in weight in assembled form, and could be built-up, using a standard kit of parts, to fulfil the same range of roles as the standard Rover 8 and to provide the same degree of weather protection. The kit included a canvas hood and frame, the standard style of windscreen, flat metal doors, standard door tops, simple side panels for the rear body and a folding tailgate.

When these items were removed, what remained was little more than a flat platform with an engine compartment in the front, seats for the crew, and wheel arches either side of a flat load platform at the rear. In this form, there was a considerable saving in weight and yet, the vehicle remained fully operational.

A total of six pre-production machines were constructed in 1966 and were put through the usual automotive trials at FVRDE.

The initial requirement was identified as being just 75 vehicles for the Royal Marines but, by 1972, it was planned that the 'lightweight'

Above: 'Lightweights' were effectively the standard military Series III short-wheelbase Land Rover and served with the British Army across the world. This example carries the coalition identfying mark used during the first Iraq War. *(ST)*

would completely replace the standard 88in (2.24m) Land Rover - by that time known as the Rover 10 - in the British Army.

Series IIA

Manufacture of the Series IIA-based vehicle started at the end of 1967, and a production example was exhibited at the Commercial Motor Show in September 1968. By the end of 1968 a total of 750 examples had been built, and the vehicle started to enter service in 1969.

There were detail differences when compared to the prototype and pre-production vehicles, the most notable of these being the reinstatement of the engine oil cooler and the use of three, rather than four straps to secure the spare wheel.

Although, officially all British Army 'lightweights' were petrol powered, a few diesel-engined examples were apparently purchased for special purposes.

By the time production was underway, the military had changed the method of describing vehicle payloads and the 'lightweight' was upgraded from 1/4 ton (254kg) to 1/2 ton (508kg), with the official designation for the basic variants being 'truck, GS (or FFR), 1/2 ton, 4x4, Rover 1'. The FFR variant used a screened 24V electrical system, but the major difference between the two models was that the there only two front seats in the FFR, the centre passenger position being replaced by a large battery box. The vehicle could also be supplied with what was described as a 'unitary radio kit' which featured a battery carrier, radio table, equipment rack and protective canopy. All of which allowed quick and easy conversion from the cargo to communications roles.

The vehicle remained in production until March 1972, by which time around 3,000 vehicles had been built, in both left- and right-hand drive

form. Very few modifications were made during the production run but, from about 1970, the headlamps were moved from the grille to the wing fronts - home market civilian Series IIA vehicles having received this modification in 1969.

Series III

In October 1971, the standard Series IIA was replaced by the Series III and this change was reflected in the 'lightweight' production line when the Series III-based machine was introduced in May 1972. Outwardly, little was changed, but there was a new type of all-synchromesh gearbox, a new type of clutch, servo-assisted brakes and a 12V alternator to replace the DC generator - the 24V machines having always been so equipped. On late-production Series IIIs the standard half-shafts and drive caps were used since the aircraft-loading width was no longer critical.

The 1/2-ton (508kg) Series III was considerably more successful than the predecessor and was used to replace existing Rover 8 and Rover 10 vehicles in all three British military services. It also became the standard short-wheelbase military Land Rover in British service, and few 88in (2.24m) standard Series IIIs were purchased.

The military registration records suggest that nearly 11,000 examples were constructed for the British services before the production line was closed in 1984, and Series III 'lightweights' were also delivered to Belgium, Brunei, Denmark, Guyana, Hong Kong, Jamaica, Indonesia, Libya and the Netherlands. The latter, along with Denmark, decided to purchase FFR 24V diesel-powered models… and modified the vehicles in various ways which did not help with performance or reliability! The Series III was never officially offered to civilian customers.

The advent of larger transport aircraft and more powerful heavy-lift helicopters meant that the vehicles were rarely seen in stripped-down form. The 'lightweight' was pretty much obsolete by the late 1980s and was eventually superseded by the Defender 90. The last examples were withdrawn from the British Army towards the end of the 1990s.

Variants

The 'lightweight' was produced as GS/utility and FFR variants.

From around 1969, a number of vehicles were retro-fitted with factory-style hardtops,

Above: A good comparison between the Series III 'lightweight', seen here with the standard 3/4-ton trailer, and the long-wheelbase Series III ambulance. *(IWM)*

Above left: A lightweights of the Royal Marines alongside a Sea King helicopter during winter in the Falkland Isles. *(IWM)*

with either a full-height rear door or a horizontally-split tailgate; some hardtops included glazed windows, others had sliding windows or were unglazed.

Around 100 examples of an anti-tank variant were produced by Marshalls of Cambridge, mounting the US Army M40A1 106mm recoiless rifle; see page 139. Examples of this were supplied to the Saudi Arabian National Guard, and to the armies of Sudan and Oman, but none entered service with the British Army.

Roles

The 88in (2.24m) 'lightweight' was considered an extremely versatile vehicle and was expected to be able to be used by troops almost wherever they were deployed and to be adapted to every conceivable role. The Honourable Artillery Company even had a fleet of highly polished

'lightweights' which could be seen towing their equally polished 25-pounder guns on ceremonial occasions.

Workshop conversions were made to small numbers of vehicles to cover the ambulance, WOMBAT anti-tank, 81mm mortar and line-laying roles. Vehicles used in Northern Ireland were frequently fitted with the 'vehicle protection kit' (VPK). This consisted of a hardtop, appliqué composite GRP or Makrolon ballistic-protection panels for the doors, floor and bonnet, an armoured shield for the windscreen, wire-mesh screens over the windows and lights; two doors were fitted at the rear, and a two-man hatch was installed in the roof.

With the addition of a snorkel and the application of suitable waterproofing, the vehicle could be made sufficiently amphibious to wade ashore from a landing craft as the Royal Marines frequently demonstrated.

Left: Before the advent of true air-portability, small vehicles could be delivered by parachute using a special stressed platform. Inevitably, if a parachute failed to deploy correctly, the vehicle would almost certainly be destroyed. Here we see long- and short-wheelbase Series IIs rigged for air dropping. *(RAFM)*

Technical specification
Half-ton 'lightweight'; 1965 to 1984

Typical nomenclature: truck, 1/2 ton, GS, FFR-24V, 4x4; FV18102; Rover 1.

Engine: Land Rover; four cylinders; 2,286cc; overhead valves; petrol; power output, 77bhp at 4,250rpm; torque, 124 lbf/ft at 2,500rpm. Diesel option also available.

Transmission: 4F1Rx2; part-time 4x4.

Steering: recirculating ball; optional steering damper on the drag link.

Suspension: live axles on multi-leaf semi-elliptical springs; hydraulic double-acting telescopic shock absorbers.

Brakes: hydraulic; drums all-round; vacuum servo-assistance on Series III models.

Construction: welded box-section steel chassis; steel-framed aluminium-panelled body with demountable panels.

Electrical system: 12V or 24V.

Dimensions

Length, 147in (3.73m) assembled; 143in (3.63m) stripped.

Width, 64in (1.6m) assembled, 60in (1.52m) stripped.

Height, 77in (1.96m) assembled, 58in (1.47m) stripped.

Wheelbase, 88in (2.24m).

Ground clearance, 8.25in (21cm).

Weight, 3,210lb (1,456kg) unladen, 4,450lb (2,018.5kg) laden; 2,660lb (1,206.6kg) minimum stripped weight.

Performance

Maximum speed, (road) 65mph (105kph); (cross country) 25mph (40kph).

Range of action, 350 miles (563km).

Approach angle, 49°;

Departure angle, 36°; (58° and 38°, respectively, in stripped down form)

Fording depth, 20in (51cm).

FV numbers
- FV18101 Truck, 1/2 ton, GS, 4x4; Rover 1
- FV18102 Truck, 1/2 ton, GS, FFR-24V, 4x4; Rover 1
- FV18103 Truck, 1/2 ton, utility, 4x4; Rover Series 3
- FV18104 Truck, 1/2 ton, utility, FFR-24V, 4x4; Rover Series 3

2.7 | 1-tonne Forward-Control '101'

Whilst the military 'lightweight' was never offered to civilian users it was, at least in part, derived from the short-wheelbase Series II and IIA chassis and thus only partially qualifies as a purpose-made military vehicle. The forward-control Land Rover - generally described as the 101 - was a different matter entirely.

Developed initially to satisfy a War Office requirement for a helicopter-portable artillery tractor to tow the 105mm light gun, carry the gun crew and a quantity of ammunition, it was totally unlike anything that Rover had offered before. It borrowed little from existing Land Rovers and, with an uncompromisingly brutal appearance, certainly had a unique look.

The 101 was not Land Rover's first attempt at constructing a forward-control truck, nor their first attempt at producing such a vehicle for the military. In 1962, a 109in (2.77m) wheelbase Series II-based forward control was launched for civilian users and was also trialled at the Fighting Vehicles Research & Development Establishment (FVRDE), although it was not purchased in quantity. Three years later, the company prototyped a 30cwt (1,524.1kg) forward-control vehicle with a 120in (3.01m) wheelbase, again to no avail. And in 1966, the Series II forward-control was fitted with a six-cylinder 2.6-litre engine, necessitating an extension of the

wheelbase to 110in (2.79m) and a change of designation to Series IIB... again, it was trialled by FVRDE but the military remained unimpressed.

It is not difficult to see why the military authorities were interested in a Land Rover which offered a larger-than-normal payload. The War Office had already identified what it described as a 'serious gap' in the future vehicle range between the 1/4 ton (254kg) and 3/4 ton (762kg) Land Rovers and the 4 ton (4,064kg) Bedford MK/MJ trucks. A War Office paper explained that 'there are many roles for which the smaller vehicles are inadequate and the larger one expensive or tactically unacceptable' and, in 1965, the authorities proposed a 1 ton (1,016kg) vehicle which, with the addition of a powered 1 ton (1,016kg) trailer, could form the basis of a 2 ton (2,032kg) power train. One of its intended roles was that of tractor for the 105mm light field gun which was too heavy to be towed by existing Land Rovers.

A year later, there were preliminary trials with an oversized, 110in (2.8m) wheelbase, 3/4 ton (762kg) bonneted 'lightweight', but only two or, perhaps, three examples were constructed and there was no series production. See page 80.

The 101 project, proper, dates from 1967 when Rover started work on constructing five forward-control 1 ton (1,016kg) military prototypes in conjunction with FVRDE. The first of these appeared in 1969 and although it generally resembled the production '10', there was a short 'boxy' bonnet projection to house the 2,995cc P5 straight-six engine. The drive-line featured selectable four-wheel drive, and ENV differentials taken from the SIIB civilian forward-control chassis.

These early forward-control prototypes were not quite what the military wanted, the six-cylinder engine presumably being under-powered when towing a gun or loaded trailer, but they did help to crystallise what was actually required. In June 1968, a General Statement of Requirements (GSR 3463) was issued which described the definitive, now metricated, 1-tonne vehicle. It was intended that it could be used as a tractor for the new 105mm light gun, as well as being able to tow a load of up to 4,000lb (1,814kg). Other possible roles included command post, Rapier and MILAN missile launcher, missile test/repair vehicle, signals office, radio repair vehicle, computer exchange unit, dry-air generator, power-supply vehicle, battery-charging truck, line layer, load carrier, and battlefield ambulance. There was also some talk of the truck being used as a mount for the EMI-designed Cymbeline mortar-locating radar system, also as a REME welding shop, but these roles were eventually withdrawn.

Demountable body panels allowed the vehicle weight to be reduced to 7,700lb (3,493kg) to allow lifting by Wessex heli-copters, and it was also air-portable in Andover and Britannia aircraft. The specification also

Above: Originally designed as a gun tractor, this is the less-common signals variant, with the so-called 'box utility' body. (ST)

Right: The prototype
101 had a short
bonnet projection
to accommodate
the original straight-
six engine. This
example mounts
Beeswing anti-
aircraft missiles.
(TM)

Above: Early
experiments were
aimed at using the
101 in conjunction
with a powered-axle
trailer. *(RMC)*

retained the requirement that the vehicle be capable of towing a powered-axle trailer (now upgraded to 3,300lb (1,947kg) capacity) via a special trailer coupling and detachable propshaft. The coupling allowed the trailer to roll through 360° without damage, and also provided up to 50° of movement in pitch and yaw.

Examples of the matching trailer were produced by Rubery Owen and Scottorn, but the concept was not continued into production for two reasons. Firstly, FVRDE discovered that the trailer could force the vehicle to jack-knife on tight downhill corners, but perhaps more importantly, the trailer could only be used with one vehicle type and this was not considered to be cost-effective.

Left: The signals body can easily be recognised by the lower roof height when compared to the ambulance. *(TM)*

But, Land Rover was not to be the 'automatic' choice, the specification was presented to the world's motor industry in August 1968 with invitations to tender. The War Office was said to be considering some 16 different vehicles for the role, including the appalling, but amphibious, US-built M561 6x6 Condec 'Gama Goat', as well as 'off-the-shelf' machines from Steyr-Puch, Toyota, Austin, International, Chrysler and Kaiser-Jeep. None of the 'off-the-shelf' vehicles met the requirements of the GSR and, in truth, there were actually only two serious contenders for the role.

The first was the Volvo-Ailsa 4140 series Laplander, an excellent 1 ton (1,016kg) 4x4 truck which had been developed for the Swedish Army during the mid-1960s, and also had the advantage of being amphibious.

The other was a heavily redeveloped version of the engineering prototype which Rover had already produced in collaboration with FVRDE. Whilst the submissions from Rover and Volvo were both considered to meet the GSR requirements in full, it appears that Rover had already made some contribution to the preparation of the GSR; so it could be argued that the competition was slightly loaded in Rover's favour.

Where the earlier Rover prototypes for the 101 had used a simplified and heavily-reinforced version of the chassis of the standard 109in (2.77m) truck, on the later prototypes and production vehicles, the chassis was a simple ladder type made up of two overlapped U steel sections welded on the vertical faces, with flat-topped side-members and intermediate supports.

Above: Marshalls of Cambridge-bodied ambulance showing the distinctive air intake grille fitted to some models. *(TM)*

Above: A standard 101 ambulance. *(PR)*

The body was constructed in much the same way as that of the 'lightweight' with removable windscreen, side and rear panels, and top. This gradually reduced the overall weight of the vehicle to below the 7,700lb (3,500kg) figure.

The urgency of the requirement ruled out the possibility of using either diesel or multi-fuel

engines but, equally, FVRDE decided that there was no suitable power unit already in service. Rover intended to use the all-aluminium Buick-derived V8 which was being planned for the Range Rover but, initially, these engines were apparently in such short supply that, at one time, a 3 litre six-cylinder Ford Falcon petrol engine

was used for development work. The Range Rover gearbox and permanent four-wheel-drive transfer case were also selected, albeit with a lower ratio low gear, coupled to heavy-duty Salisbury axles incorporating larger half-shafts than standard; an inter-axle differential lock was also fitted. The competing Volvo was fitted with differential locks on the individual axles, but these had not been specified by FVRDE and so were not fitted by Rover.

The suspension was thoroughly conventional, with live axles on semi-elliptical tapered multi-leaf springs with an anti-roll bar at front. Double-acting telescopic hydraulic shock absorbers were fitted all round. The wheels were of 16in diameter, with a unique six-stud mounting and were fitted with big 9.00x16 bar-grip tyres.

Approach and departure angles were excellent, and the vehicle was said to be capable of 79mph (127km/h) on the road. The low axle ratios (5.57:1), combined with the lower gear in the transfer case, gave an astonishing 74:1 low gear, almost twice the figure of the standard Land Rover.

Many of the production vehicles were fitted with a centre-mounted Nokken capstan winch, fitted to the outside of the left-hand chassis rail

and driven by a power take-off on the transfer case. The winch could be driven by any of the forward gears and in either of the transfer-case ratios. The winch could be rigged to allow either forward or backward pulls.

Prototypes

A total of 10 prototype vehicles were constructed in 1970 for trials, at a cost of £3,500 each; of these, six were to be trialled by FVRDE, including arctic and tropical trials, where the cost of £25,000 was borne by FVRDE rather than the manufacturer. The remainder were intended for user trials, with three delivered to the School of Artillery for trials with the 105mm gun.

Mock-ups were also produced which allowed concurrent development of the various equipment and installations. The trials were scheduled to end in early 1972 with the winning vehicle going into production immediately.

Production

The Land Rover emerged as the clear winner and was put into production as the FV19000

Above: GS 101 hitched to the towed Rapier surface to air anti-aircraft missile system. (PR)

Far left: The Vampire signals variant can easily be identified by the differently-shaped roof. It was believed to have been used as a re-broadcast vehicle. (PR)

series; the first production variant was the GS/artillery tractor.

Rover chose the Commercial Motor Show of 1972 to announce that they had secured the contract, but both the Volvo and the Land Rover had already appeared in public when they were included in the 1971 exhibition of military vehicles at FVRDE's Chertsey, Surrey trials establishment.

Production did not actually commence until 1975, with the first vehicles being delivered to the British Army the same year. The vehicle remained in production for three years, and the total produced for the British Army was 2,129 vehicles, of which 520 were bodied as ambulances. A further 127 vehicles were supplied to the RAF.

The 101 was also supplied to the armies of Australia, Egypt, Iran and Luxembourg and was also evaluated by Canada and others. Total production was 2,669 vehicles.

Variants

There were four production variants in total - GS, ambulance, and two types of signals body - with both right- and left-hand drive vehicles

Below: The signals body known as the 'box utility' was built by Laird of Anglesey. *(PW)*

being produced. Although the vehicle was designated as the FV19000 series, by the time it entered service the 'FV' numbering system had more-or-less fallen into disuse and, despite a dozen or so numbers being allocated to the series, only the ambulances appear to have actually been given 'FV' numbers.

As well as providing a high-performance off-road general service vehicle which could carry 10 personnel with equipment the GS variant fulfilled the original role of tractor for the 105mm light gun. It was also used as a prime mover and tracking unit for the Rapier anti-aircraft missile system, as a mortar carrier and as a mount for the MILAN anti-tank missile. The vehicle was also trialled with the British Aircraft Corporation's Beeswing missile system which deployed a battery of six Swingfire anti-tank missiles; see page 136.

The ambulance was developed by Marshalls of Cambridge and was fitted with a large box-shaped insulated rear body capable of accommodating two or four stretcher cases or, alternatively, one or two stretcher cases plus four seated, or eight seated casualties. Ventilation and heating facilities were provided in the cab and body and there was an oxygen supply in the rear. Ambulances intended for the RAF crash-rescue role also included engine pre-heating facilities, a battery trickle charger and a radio installation. All of the ambulances were apparently converted from standard GS vehicles where, aside from the body, modifications were restricted to the use of uprated front and rear shock absorbers.

A similar body - known as the 'box utility' - was designed by Lairds of Anglesey for the signals and electronics repair variant, with vehicles also being converted from the GS role. A second signals body variant, known as Vampire, was believed to have been used as a re-broadcast vehicle. This can be readily identified by the single side door and differently-shaped roof.

REME also converted the vehicle for forward repair teams by fitting a two-man enclosed cab and a small HIAB hydraulic crane and winch. A number of signals vehicles were converted to biological agent detection vans during the first Gulf War.

Technical specification
1 tonne forward control 101; 1972 to 1974
Nomenclature: truck, 1 tonne, 4x4, GS, forward control; FV19000 series; Land Rover.

Engine: Rover; eight cylinders in V formation; 3,528cc; petrol; overhead valves; power output, 128bhp at 5,000rpm; torque, 205 lbf/ft at 3,000rpm.
Transmission: 4F1Rx2; full-time 4x4; positive lock on inter axle differential.
Steering: recirculating ball, worm and nut; Woodhead steering damper.
Suspension: live axles on semi-elliptical tapered multi-leaf springs; anti-roll bar at front; double-acting telescopic hydraulic shock absorbers, uprated on the ambulance variant.
Brakes: servo-assisted dual-circuit hydraulic, drums all-round.
Construction: welded box-section steel chassis with steel-framed aluminium-panelled body; body panels demountable to reduce overall weight.
Electrical system: 12V, or 24V.

Dimensions
Length, 162in (4.1m).
Width, 72in (1.83m).
Height, 84in (2.13m) soft-top variants, 94in (2.4m) hardtop variants.
Wheelbase, 101in (2.57m).
Ground clearance, 10in (25.4cm).
Weight, 4,233lb (1,920kg) unladen, 6,840lb (3,102.6kg) laden; 3,500lb (1,588kg) minimum stripped weight.

Performance
Maximum speed, (road) 62mph (99.8kg); (cross country) 25mph (40kph).
Range of action, 350 miles (563km).
Approach angle, 50°.
Departure angle, 45°.
Fording depth, 24in (61cm).

FV numbers
- FV19009 Truck, 1 tonne, 4x4, ambulance, 4 stretcher, LHD; Land Rover
- FV19010 Truck, 1 tonne, 4x4, ambulance, 4 stretcher; Land Rover

Other variants do not appear to have been issued with FV numbers.

Above:
Photographed during the Falklands Victory Parade, the soft tops have been removed from these 101s to allow the crowd to better see the crews. These vehicles are doing exactly what they were designed for and are towing 105mm light guns. *(IWM)*

2.8 | Oddballs and Prototypes

No-one can deny the extraordinary success of the Land Rover. Although conceived as an agricultural machine, early adoption by the British Army and subsequent use throughout almost an a 60-year service life has ensured the vehicle a place in military history.

It would be curious if the Land Rover designers had not found themselves wandering down the odd developmental by-way during that time... some military, some civilian.

Whilst some of these vehicles, such as the Hover Rover, were definitely 'non-starters', others provided important lessons for vehicles that were to follow.

Command car

In 1952, the War Office asked Land Rover to produce a prototype for a purpose-designed military command car.

As with the civilian Tickford estate car of 1948, the basis of the vehicle was the standard 80in (2.02m) Series I, carrying a full-width four-door utilitarian body with seats for six - two in the front and two on a rear-facing bench, with two more inward facing seats at the extreme rear, all of the rear seats being grouped around a map table. The backrest to the rear bench seat could be swung across to provide a forward-facing seat. Sliding glass was fitted into all four doors and the rear-most side windows. The one-piece fixed windscreen was held in place by a rubber moulding.

A large stowage bin was bolted to the hinged rear door and a luggage rack was mounted on the roof. This was reached by means of a step on the left-hand rear body panel.

The vehicle could not be described as attractive. The combination of a considerable rear overhang and the additional width beyond the scuttle, gave it a very uncomfortable appearance, and the flat-sided body had little in common with the standard Land Rover front end. The fixed, shallow screen, particularly, had the effect of giving the vehicle excessive width.

The prototype vehicle was put into a head-to-head trial against a mock-up heavy utility on the FV1600 series Humber 1 ton (1,016kg) chassis but, again, there was to be no series production... of either the Rover or the Humber.

Above and left:
In 1952, Land Rover produced this one-off four-door hard-top command car on the standard Series I chassis. There was no series production and the fate of the vehicle is not known. *(PW)*

Right: The backrest to the rear seat of the command car could be swung either way to allow the use of a radio set or map table in the extreme rear. *(PW)*

Below: The so-called 'fat light-weight' was an attempt at producing a more powerful vehicle which could also be stripped for air portability. Only two or three examples were constructed. *(TM)*

3/4-ton 'lightweight'

In the mid-1960s, Land Rover produced what was virtually a 3/4 ton (762kg) version of the military 'lightweight', and submitted two, or maybe three, examples to the Fighting Vehicles Research & Development Establishment (FVRDE) for assessment trials.

In appearance this was a fat 'lightweight', sharing the same flat-panelled demountable two-door open bodywork, flat front and high cut-away wings. It was powered by Rover's 3-litre six-cylinder 110bhp petrol engine, in combination with a four-speed gearbox and two-speed transfer case. The heavy-duty, wide-track ENV axles, as used on the civilian forward-

control models, were suspended front and rear on semi-elliptical springs and the wheelbase was 110in (2.79m). Like the forward-control 101, it was intended to be used with a powered trailer driven via a second transfer case at the rear of the chassis, giving a choice of 6x6, 6x4 and 6x2 configurations.

Although this particular project was not progressed, it did help to determine the design parameters for the forward-control 101 (see page 72).

1.5-ton forward-control

FVRDE had already trialled at least one of the Series IIB 1 ton (1,016kg) forward-control trucks in the mid-1960s and it was possibly this which led to the requirement for what was described as a '30cwt (1,524kg) GS load carrier'. Both Austin and Land Rover offered similar prototypes for assessment during 1965, whilst Bedford and Commer produced normal-control vehicles for the same role. All were exhibited at the 1966 exhibition of military vehicles at Chertsey.

The Land Rover submission used a widened version of the cab of the Series II with a sharply cut-off short bonnet covering a Perkins 6.354 model six-cylinder diesel engine. More than 12in

(30.5cm) wider than the Series II, the cab sat high on over-sized 11.00x16 wheels. The wheelbase was extended to 120in (3.01m) and the track measured 8.5in (22cm) wider than the standard vehicle. The overall weight of the completed vehicle was a considerable 7,460lb (3,384kg) and, presumably, every bhp of power produced by the 5,800cc diesel engine was required, in conjunction with a five-speed gearbox and two-speed transfer case, to achieve the maximum speed of 40mph (64kph).

This was another of those projects which slipped quietly away and the role, as envisaged, was never fulfilled.

Hover Rover

The 'Hover Rover' might well be the most outrageous special Land Rover of all time. Hovercraft were all the rage in the early 1960s, and the military authorities were as keen as anyone to exploit the extraordinary ability of such vehicles to cross both solid terrain, almost regardless of condition and topography, and water. What could be better than a Land Rover which exhibited the properties of a hovercraft?

Vickers, who had supplied the first commercial hovercraft in the summer of 1962, had actually

Above and overleaf: The 'Hover Rover' attempted to exploit the legendary go-anywhere abilities of the Land Rover with the versatility of the air-cushion hovercraft. Two or three prototypes were produced in different configurations, but the vehicle did not enter production. (TM)

announced the Hover Rover a month or two earlier, in May 1962. It consisted of a 109in (2.77m) Series II, dating from 1961, with a second engine installed on the rear load bed, driving a pair of vertically-mounted lift fans… an inflatable rubber skirt was fitted around the perimeter of the vehicle and there were modifications to virtually every body panel. Unlike most hovercraft, the vehicle was actually still driven by its wheels; the hover fans simply provided enough lift to prevent the weight of the machine from bogging down on soft and marshy ground.

It was trialled, and famously filmed, by FVRDE between 1962 and 1963, but there were no purchases.

Little is known about a second such vehicle, which more closely resembled a conventional hovercraft, being powered by a horizontally-mounted single large lift fan. Again, it was certainly tested by the military authorities, but never entered service.

Llama

Dating from the mid-1980s, the unsuccessful Llama project was an attempt to provide a more modern and 'civilised' vehicle to replace the forward-control 101.

The first prototypes appeared in the period 1985 to 1986. Bearing little resemblance to any contemporary Land Rover, it was a purposeful looking 2-tonne truck with a two-door glass-fibre composite tilt cab. Mechanical components were derived from the 110, with power provided by the Buick-derived V8 petrol engine driving what, by then, had become the standard Land Rover permanent all-wheel-drive transmission, consisting of a five-speed gearbox and two-speed transfer case with centre lockable differential. A power take-off was included to drive an under-floor winch. Heavy-duty Salisbury axles were used with coil-spring suspension.

Cargo, gun tractor and box van prototypes were produced. All were trialled at Chertsey and Farnborough, in some cases being tested directly against the 4x4 and 6x6 Stonefield vehicles. Nothing came of the project... or of the Stonefield for that matter!

Right: The standard civilian Series IIB forward-control vehicle was also tested at FVRDE in the mid-1960s. This example has been fitted with an experimental Archimedes screw-type load/traction assistance equipment. *(RA)*

Centre and below: The Llama project was an attempt to provide a more modern and 'civilised' vehicle to replace the forward-control 101. It was trialed against prototypes from Stonefield and Reynolds-Boughton. The vehicle did not enter production. *(TM)*

Left and below:
Land Rover's Special Projects Department was adept at producing one-off vehicles for specific purpose and, where a 6x6 chassis was called for, examples were available from both Hotspur and SMC Engineering of Bristol. Little is known of the HiAB-equipped machine but it was clearly trialled for possible military use. *(BM)*

section three
Special Applications

3.1 | Special Forces Vehicles

The whole special forces 'thing' - and, of course, the legendary 'Pink Panthers' - started with the specially-equipped Jeeps which David Stirling's Special Air Service Regiment (SASR) used during the North Africa campaign in 1942 to 1943.

Previous page:
Constructed by Marshalls of Cambridge, the iconic Series IIA-based 'Pink Panther' is typical of long-range patrol vehicles, carrying weapons, stores, spare parts, fuel and whatever is needed to allow the crew to survive behind enemy lines for days at a time.
(PC)

These, in turn, led to the development of the SAS Series I Land Rovers which replaced the Jeeps in the early 1950s, and then to the Series IIA 'Pink Panthers' and the Defender-based special operations and multi-role combat vehicles of today.

Actually, that is not quite true because the SAS was preceded by the Long Range Desert Group (LRDG), which originally used well-equipped, heavily-armed American Chevrolet light trucks to ambush enemy convoys and raid supply dumps. The LRDG's patrols carried sufficient fuel, water and firepower to allow them to exist on their own resources for days at a time. The Jeep did not enter the picture until 1942 when the success of the LRDG's operations led to the formation of Special Air Services Brigade. The Brigade was equipped with a fleet of 16 modified Jeeps.

The SAS was disbanded in 1945, then reformed during the Malayan Emergency of the early 1950s. By this time the special Jeeps were long

since obsolete and, although there had been experiments with heavily-armed Champs in the early 1950s, in 1955 the SAS commissioned a heavily-armed patrol vehicle based on the Series I.

Series I SAS vehicles

Officially described as 'truck, 1/4 ton, 4x4, SAS, Rover Mk 3; FV18063', the first post-war SAS patrol vehicle was basically a modified 86in (2.18m) Series I cargo vehicle.

Mechanical changes were minimal, comprising little more than the use of higher-rate springs to enable the additional load to be carried. The doors and windscreen were removed and there was no canvas top or frame. A large auxiliary fuel tank was fitted inside the body, beneath a single rear-facing seat for the radio operator/rear gunner. The centre section of the front seat was removed, and the passenger seat was modified and repositioned. A radio was carried in the rear.

Above: Bristling with guns and hung about with supplies and personal kit, the Jeep used by the SAS in World War Two became the model for all special forces vehicles. *(PW)*

Left: The SAS used the converted short-wheelbase Land Rovers Series I for the same purpose in the mid-1950s. *(PW)*

Above and right:
Additional views of the SAS Series I. The vehicle mounts twin-Vickers K machine guns at the front, and a .50 calibre heavy machinegun at the rear; a Bren gun is stowed beside the passenger seat. Note also the sun compass mounted on the centre of the scuttle. *(PW)*

Standard armaments included two 7.62mm general-purpose machine guns (GPMG) on a coupled mount at the front, where they could be operated by the co-driver and a Browning .30 calibre machine gun at the rear. A third GPMG was normally stowed beside the driver.

The role dictated that considerable additional equipment needed to be carried, including jerrycans for fuel and water. These were stowed on the reinforced front bumper and inside the vehicle. Additional stowage bins and lockers were also fitted wherever practicable, and the spare wheel was carried on a bracket mounted on the front bumper.

The first vehicle was converted in April 1955, with the work being carried out in the Chertsey workshops of the Fighting Vehicles Research & Development Establishment (FVRDE). Two more were produced in January 1956, and a further six in February 1957. Automotive trials on the original conversion were conducted at FVRDE in late 1957, before the vehicle was returned to the War Office for air-dropping trials.

A number of 88in (2.24m) chassis were also converted to this role in a similar manner and remained in service until 1967, when the Series I

Left: Early Series II-based 'Pink Panther' prototype undergoing trials with the SAS Regiment, probably photographed in 1968. *(RA)*

was replaced by the long-wheelbase Series IIA… the iconic 'Pink Panther'.

Series IIA 'Pink Panther'

The military requirements for what was officially known as 'truck, 3/4 ton, general service, SAS, 4x4, Rover 11; FV18064' - the legendary 'Pink Panther' - were drawn up by the SAS Regiment in 1964 and were derived from experience gained on operations with the Series I vehicles. What the SAS wanted had changed little since 1942… a reliable long-range patrol vehicle for deep penetration missions, usually behind enemy lines, often in desert conditions. 'Long range' meant that the vehicle had to be able to carry a three-man crew, along with weapons for attack and self-defence, plus radio communications equipment, and large quantities of fuel, water and other supplies.

During the early 1960s, the Regiment had produced, perhaps 27, prototypes on the Series II chassis in conjunction with the Royal Electrical & Mechanical Engineers (REME). Unfortunately, ex-works performance of the Series II was not able to provide the necessary reliability when fully loaded with weapons,

ammunition, crew and supplies. It was decided that development of a more highly-modified vehicle be handed over to FVRDE and the Regiment supplied a list the equipment which it expected to be carried in the vehicle. FVRDE's challenge was to develop a vehicle which could do this without being unduly heavy or without sacrificing strength in crucial areas. The existing vehicles were also made available for inspection together with a description of their shortcomings.

In December 1965, FVRDE issued a 'statement of requirements', which included 23

Above: The production 'Pink Panthers' were based on the Series IIA chassis, with delivery of the first vehicle taking place in October 1968. All were originally painted in the standard Deep Bronze Green. *(PW)*

Above: The Defender-based remote area patrol vehicle, produced by Glover Webb, was similar to the Marshall's-built desert patrol vehicle. *(ST)*

Right: The heavy machine gun position on a rapid deployment vehicle. *(PW)*

modifications, mostly to the existing equipment and stowage facilities. Using a long-wheelbase Series II as a basis, FVRDE's engineers set to work to produce a prototype.

REME had already demonstrated that heavy-duty springs and shock absorbers together with one-piece wheels mounting 9.00x15 sand tyres could help to overcome failures in these areas as well as increasing mobility. These modifications were retained. The chassis was reinforced at critical stress points, and stone guards were welded to the differential housings. A hydraulic steering damper was fitted. There were two asbestos-wrapped 100 gallon (454.6 litre) long-range fuel tanks, which allowed the vehicles to achieve an average operating range of 1,500 miles (2,414km). Expansion tanks were also fitted which allowed for a 10% increase in volume.

No changes were made to the engine or transmission, and the vehicles retained the standard 12V electrical system, with a single battery. An auxiliary 'ignition only' switch was fitted which prevented accidental operation of lights during black-out driving. A black-out driving light was fitted on the right-hand front wing. Additional power-supply sockets were fitted to the rear bulkhead.

There were no doors, windscreen, or top, and a folding pannier was mounted at the rear. The passenger seat was fitted to a raised platform, and additional seats were mounted over the rear wheel arches. The spare wheel was moved to a near-horizontal position on the front bumper.

The vehicles bristled with armaments. The standard weapons issue included two 7.62mm GPMGs, a Carl Gustav 84mm recoilless anti-tank gun, and four sets of smoke dischargers. Stowage facilities were provided for the crew's standard-issue self-loading rifles (SLR) in sheet-metal holsters on the front wing side panels.

Above: Beautifully-restored Land Rover Series I as used by the SAS. (PR)

Above and right:
Although not necessarily pink in colour, all Marshalls of Cambridge built Series IIA to SAS specifications vehicles were known as 'Pink Panthers'. Enthusiasts restoring such a vehicle can spend years locating the various items of on-board equipment.
(PC [top] PR [right])

Ammunition and grenade stowage facilities were placed between the front seats and on both sides of the rear compartment.

Other essential equipment included Larkspur A43 (ground-to-air) and A123 (morse) radios, sun compass, theodolite, and standard magnetic compass. A machete was stowed behind the rear seat, first-aid equipment, fire extinguishers and water container racks were carried inside the body. Sand channels and pioneer tools were carried externally.

By May 1967 the development work was complete and a final specification was prepared. Long-time defence contractor Marshalls of Cambridge was given the task of turning the 'paper and prototype' requirement into reality and constructing 72 production examples. The first vehicle, now based on the Series IIA 109in (2.77m) chassis, was ready for inspection in August 1968 and, on 2 October 1968, the SAS took delivery of this first vehicle, with most of the remainder following during 1969.

A fully-loaded 'Pink Panther' weighed almost 1,000lb (454kg) more than the equivalent standard Rover 11 and while the chassis, suspension and axle housings appear to have been able to withstand this kind of loading, half-shaft failure was a regular fact of life; spare shafts were generally carried when the vehicles were in active service.

Half-shaft failures aside, the vehicles were considered to be reliable and more than capable of carrying out the task for which they had been constructed. The standard operating procedure was developed in Oman where the vehicles usually went out on patrol in threes - the lead and rear vehicles would be equipped for attack or reconnaissance, while the third would carry mechanical spares such as starter motors, generators, coils, etc. Operations were also carried out in Belize, Northern Ireland and Kenya.

Despite operational losses, most of the vehicles enjoyed an almost 20 year service life, finally being replaced by the Defender 110 based special operations vehicles during the early 1990s.

The distinctive pink colour was applied to the vehicles used in the Oman Dhofar operation,

Above: Dating from the late 1980s, the SAS desert patrol vehicle was based on the Defender 110. All were constructed by Marshalls of Cambridge. *(TM)*

Above: Easily identified by the distinctive square-tube brush guard, the special operations vehicle was originally designed to provide the US Army Rangers with a rapid-reaction, air-portable all-terrain weapons platform. *(TM)*

being dubbed 'Pink Panthers' in tribute to the elusive jewel thief in the 1963 Peter Sellers film of that name. Whilst there are almost as many stories as to why pink was selected as a suitable camouflage as there were vehicles constructed, it is worth pointing out that not all 'Pink Panthers' were pink! All of the vehicles started life being painted in the standard military Deep Bronze Green and some probably stayed that way for their entire service life, while others were painted in standard olive drab with the familiar black 'shadow' camouflage.

Desert patrol vehicle

The 'Pink Panther' was effectively a private development… Land Rover supplied standard production vehicles, which were modified by Marshalls of Cambridge. Land Rover made such vehicles available as a standard option with the introduction of the special operations vehicle

(SOV) in 1992, and the multi-role combat vehicle (MRCV) in 1993.

Actually, there was also a 'missing link'. In the late1980s, heavily-modified Defender 110 'desert patrol vehicles' (DPV) started to enter British Army service. Superficially resembling the 'Pink Panthers', the DPV lacked doors, a windscreen, top and frame. The distinctive body was that of the civilian high-capacity pick-up truck. An external roll-over bar was fitted behind the front seats. There were additional fuel tanks, as well as generous stowage capacity for additional petrol and water jerrycans, ammunition and personal kit. A pair of 7.62mm GPMGs were mounted in the rear, with a third pedestal-mounted on the scuttle; there were also bumper-mounted smoke dischargers.

The standard power unit was the 3.5-litre V8 petrol engine, and the suspension was uprated.

Like the 'Pink Panther', the DPV was assembled by Marshalls of Cambridge,

Special operations vehicle

Next came the 'special operations vehicle' (SOV), originally designed to provide the US Army Rangers with a rapid-reaction, air-portable all-terrain weapons platform. Believing that the ubiquitous HMMWV (Humvee) was too large, the Rangers had been impressed by the performance of the British Army's Defenders during the first Iraq War and saw the SOV as a replacement for the M151A2 gun Jeep.

In 1991, Land Rover was approached with a specification for a vehicle which the Rangers believed would suit their needs. As with the DPV, it was based on the long-wheelbase four-door Defender 110, and was first seen in public at the 1992 Eurosatory Show in Paris. The Rangers took delivery of 60 examples in 1993, and the SOV was also offered to other defence customers.

The Rangers' SOV, or RSOV, was powered by the 300 Tdi four-cylinder 2.5 litre turbo-charged diesel engine, but the 3.5-litre V8 petrol engine was also offered. The permanent four-wheel drive system, transmission and long-travel coil-spring suspension were based on the standard Defender. Users were able to choose either a 24V 90Ah or 12V 65Ah electrical system, with optional radio suppression. There were no doors, windscreen or hood but, of course, there were considerable additional stowage facilities for ammunition, fuel, water also other tools and equipment.

A prominent feature of the design was the combined roll bar and weapons mount. Suggested armaments included two 30mm ASP-30 machine guns mounted in tandem at the rear, together with a third machine gun on the scuttle alongside the driver. The vehicle could also mount the Mk 19 40mm mortar launcher, 50mm or 81mm mortar, 0.50 calibre

Above: The multi-role combat vehicle, or rapid deployment vehicle was initially available using the Defender 90, 110 or 130 chassis and incorporated a machine gun ring mount on the roll cage. *(TM)*

Above: The rapid deployment vehicle on the 90 or 110in Wolf Defender or standard military Defender chassis. *(PR)*

heavy machine gun, AT-4 Stinger, or Carl Gustav 84mm recoilless rifle - the latter often described as the 'Ranger anti-armor weapon system' (RAAWS).

The vehicle was operated by a crew of three, driver, gunner, and leader/gunner, although Land Rover claimed that the crew capacity was actually six men in the personnel carrier role.

Designed to be air-portable inside either a C-130 Hercules or CH-47 Chinook and EH-101 helicopters, the SOV could also be sling-loaded underneath a Chinook or Blackhawk, or para-dropped on a suitable platform. Lashing points allowed under-slinging from standard NATO medium-lift helicopters such as Sea King or Puma.

Rapid deployment vehicle

In 1993, Land Rover showed the 'multi-role combat vehicle' (MRCV) at the British Army Equipment Exhibition (BAEE), Aldershot. Developed partly in conjunction with Longline, who had produced the 'buggies' favoured by the SAS, the MRCV was also derived from the Defender.

It was originally demonstrated on the short-wheelbase Defender 90, but users could also choose the Defender 110 or 130 platform.

Left: Now in private hands, this was the prototype for the US Rangers special operations vehicle. (ST)

Below: Rapid deployment vehicle mounting a MILAN anti-tank missile launcher. (PW)

The MRCV was subsequently renamed the 'rapid deployment vehicle' (RDV) and the option of using the Defender 130 chassis was discontinued.

The RDV was intended to provide maximum versatility, acting either as a weapons platform or reconnaissance vehicle. The modular construction enabled the vehicle to be converted to one of seven distinct roles, including pedestal mount, MILAN anti-tank platform, multi-purpose ring mount, and personnel or cargo carrier. Conversion from one role to another was quickly effected using only hand tools, and no modifications were required which would have compromised the vehicle's ability to carry out general service duties when not required for operational duties.

In the weapons platform role, a 360° ring mount was mounted on the roll bar, which could also be used to equip the vehicle with a 40mm grenade launcher, GIAT 20mm cannon, L1A1 0.5in Browning heavy machine gun, or 7.62mm GPMG. Pedestal mounts could also be

fitted to the scuttle or to the rear of the vehicle for an 0.5 in Browning, 40mm grenade launcher, or GIAT 20mm cannon. A 7.62mm GPMG could also be mounted anywhere on the rear roll cage. In the MILAN anti-tank (ATGW) configuration, the vehicle carried a complement of six missiles.

The RDV could also accept the 'weapons mount installation kit' (WMIK) which was developed for use with the British Army's Defender XD 110 models. The base vehicle only required minor modification, and the WMIK was easily fitted in the field using hand tools.

To enhance stability when used as a gun mount, a lock-out system could be fitted to the suspension, using hydraulic dampers which operated instantaneously from the cab once the vehicle had come to a halt.

The rear cargo area could accept a palletised load, and was provided with tie-down points. A large rear bustle was fitted to provide additional stowage facilities.

Like the SOV, there was a choice of electrical systems, with users able to choose between a 65Ah 12V system, or single or twin 24V 50Ah alternators. Optional radio suppression facilities were also available.

The RDV also offered users the same para-dropping and air-portability options as the SOV.

Above: D Squadron, the Household cavalry Regiment, in their Scimitar Armoured Reconnaisance Vehicle (left), hand over their area responsibility to the 1st Battalion, the Parachute Regiment, in their WMIC (Weapon Mounting Infantry Carrying) vehicle, near Basra. *(Crown Copyright)*

Left and far left: Defenders and Wolf Defenders are extensively used in Iraq and Afghanistan. The coloured louvred panel evident on both the light tank and the patrol vehicle to the left is a 'friend or foe' recognition device. *(PW)*

3.2 | Ambulances

During World War Two the Jeep provided a suitable platform for what was known as a field expedient ambulance, albeit the stretcher carrying arrangements were, necessarily, somewhat makeshift.

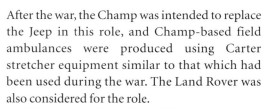

After the war, the Champ was intended to replace the Jeep in this role, and Champ-based field ambulances were produced using Carter stretcher equipment similar to that which had been used during the war. The Land Rover was also considered for the role.

The projected field expedient ambulances were abandoned but, when this happened, it was the Land Rover rather than the Champ which was selected for a purpose-designed military ambulance and it has remained in this role to the present day.

Series I field ambulance

The field expedient ambulance had a splendid pedigree. Jeeps had been used in this role during World War Two using a variety of different systems, known variously as the Edwards, the Carter, the Australian airborne, and the Janes. The Carter system was selected as the basis for a post-war field ambulance.

The Carter system produced a simple field ambulance from a 1/4 ton (254kg) utility vehicle without compromising its basic role, and the equipment could be removed once no longer required. The system had been trial-fitted to the Champ and the Wolseley Mudlark, so it must have appeared logical to also use the same kit on the short-wheelbase Land Rover. In late 1957, the Fighting Vehicles Research & Development Executive (FVRDE) undertook the ambulance conversion of an 86in (2.18m) wheelbase Series I testing, not only the vehicle, but also checking the suitability of the stretcher kit which had been designed for use with the Champ.

FVRDE hoped that the equipment could be standardised between the Champ and the Land Rover, and two trial installations were made. The first attempted to use all of the brackets and fittings available in the kit designed for use with the Champ - this necessitated considerable modification to the Land Rover

body. The second avoided modifications to the body, but required new mounting and support brackets to be developed expressly for the Land Rover.

In the interests of optimum standardisation and simplicity of installation, the second course was considered the most practical. This meant that the only elements of the Champ kit used on the Land Rover were the front supporting cross-member and the stretcher rails - the fixing brackets, cross-member supports, canopy, and canopy supports were all unique.

As installed, the stretcher equipment consisted of two pairs of channel-section rails carried on brackets attached to the rear body, and supported on a tubular cross-member just behind the front seats - the cross-member, in turn, was supported on a pair of uprights fitted to the inner wheel arches. The stretchers were simply slid into position along the rails and secured in place by webbing straps.

The rails and stretchers, protruded more than two feet behind the vehicle and were protected by a snout-like canvas extension to the rear of the canopy. Even with the canopy in the fully buttoned-up position, cut-outs had to be provided to allow the stretcher handles to protrude outside.

In both trial installations, the forward ends of the stretcher rails were supported on a tubular cross-member but the location of this cross-member, immediately behind the front seat backs, prevented the normal spare-wheel position from being used. This was overcome by relocating the wheel to the bonnet, where there was 'a slight impairment of the driver's vision'. It was suggested that it might be better to simply slip the wheel under the stretchers. The tailgate could still be opened, although of course it remained in the closed position whilst the stretcher gear was in use.

After installation - in practice this would have been considered as a 'unit modification',

Above: Originally derived from the RAF mountain rescue ambulances, the distinctive 2/4 stretcher body was built by several manufacturers, and appeared, more or less unchanged, on Series I, II and III chassis. *(RAFM)*

requiring about 16 man-hours' work - the Land Rover was subjected to 'automotive trials'. These trials consisted of nothing more than 100 miles (161km) on the Chertsey pavé and boulder courses, and 200 miles (323km) on the Bagshot Heath, Surrey cross-country course.

With the stretcher gear installed, the vehicle could carry two patients and a two-man crew. For the duration of the trials, it was loaded with the full complement - driver, front-seat passenger and two stretcher assemblies, although the report did not state whether or not the stretchers were loaded. Aside from the webbing straps, it is hard to see what measures were available to prevent the stretchers from sliding about when the going got a little rough.

No problems were encountered during the trials with either the vehicle or the stretcher installation and the vehicle was said to handle 'satisfactorily' although it was said that the standard Land Rover suspension led to a ride of a 'very low order of comfort'. It was also pointed out that the inner handles of the stretchers frequently made contact with the driver's shoulders which was said to be 'uncomfortable', particularly under rough cross-country conditions'. The only way to prevent this

Left: Australian military Land Rovers can be recognised by the cut-away front wings and by the large brush guard. The big, box-shaped body on this Series II is similar to that used on British ambulances but provides more headroom. (*RAFM*)

happening was to move the stretchers further to the rear… which resulted in an even greater degree of discomfort to any occupants of the stretchers, because even more of the weight was behind the rear axle.

The vehicle was then transferred to the Royal Army Medical Corps (RAMC) Field Training School for user trials but it is very unlikely that the vehicles were ever really used in anger. Indeed, FVRDE's report concluded with the words 'as a compromise method for evacuating stretcher cases from a forward area under rough conditions of travel, the ride provided for a casualty by this installation is just tolerable'.

Mountain rescue ambulances

During World War Two, the Royal Air Force trained pilots in low-level flying techniques in the isolated and mountainous areas of Wales and, inevitably there were difficulties in finding and evacuating any survivors of downed aircraft, regardless of whether or not they were injured. In 1942, to help overcome this problem, Flight-Lieutenant F. W. Graham, who was based at RAF Llandwrog near Caenarvon, North Wales

established the first dedicated RAF mountain rescue service. A Jeep was used as a scouting vehicle, with Humber trucks to effect the rescues. The team picked up its first casualty in July 1943 and, within a year, more than 30 aircrew had been located and evacuated.

Responsibility for the rescue work passed to the Air Ministry in 1944, and the original team was relocated to Valley on the Isle of Anglesey, by 1950 there were nine teams at work. The Jeep retained its pivotal role in the rescue teams, but was now supplemented by Humber 4x4 ambulances and four-wheel drive trucks.

By the mid-1950s it was obvious that the Jeep was obsolete, and the RAF drew up a specification for a purpose-designed mountain rescue vehicle to be constructed on a long-wheelbase Series I chassis. With the combination of all-wheel drive and a spacious ambulance body, it was hoped that the Land Rover could fulfil the search and rescue roles of the Jeep, the ambulance and the accompanying trucks.

The first batch of 11 vehicles was supplied in 1956, with another 14 a year later.

The chassis selected for the role was the 107in (2.72m) long-wheelbase design - the Rover Mk 4.

Opposite page:
The Carter stretcher gear had originally been designed to allow World War Two Jeeps to be converted to field ambulance form. It was subsequently adapted for both the Land Rover and the Austin Champ and saw limited service. (*TM*)

Above: A standard RAF mountain rescue ambulance on a Series II chassis. *(PW)*

No changes were made to the technical specification, and the engine was the standard 1,997cc four-cylinder 52bhp petrol unit driving through a four-speed gearbox and two-speed transfer case. Despite the additional demands for electric power, the standard 12V system was retained.

At the rear, there was a full-width box-shaped insulated aluminium body, with a domed Luton cab roof, initially constructed by Bonallack & Sons of Basildon, Essex. Small, shuttered windows were installed high in the body sides towards the rear and there were windows in the rear doors. A hot-water interior heating system was installed, with twin blowers to distribute heat around the interior. Inside, the body provided accommodation for a driver and medical officer in the cab, and either six seated cases, two stretcher cases and an attendant, or three seated patients together with a stretcher case and an attendant. Two bunk-like stretchers were carried on fixed frames running along the sides of the body. There was no direct access from the cab, but there were side-hinged double doors at the rear, with a full-width fold-down step.

External lockers were fitted on either side ahead of the rear wheel arches.

With an overall length of 190in (4.8m), compared to 183in (4.67m) for the standard long-wheelbase cargo vehicle, combined with a height of 90in (2.3m), an increase in width of 10in (25.4cm), and a huge rear over-hang, the vehicle looked decidedly over-bodied. However, the body length was actually determined by the dimensions of the standard NATO stretcher, and even the front seats had to be moved forward to provide sufficient clearance.

When the Series I was replaced by the Series II in 1958, production simply continued using the long-wheelbase Series II chassis, then the Series IIA, and the Series III.

Aside from the obvious changes in the appearance of the front end of the Series II vehicles, there were important visual changes to the rear body. These included a reduction in overall height to allow transport in heavy-lift aircraft of the period, the addition of a second side window in the rear body, placed towards the front end, and the inclusion of an angled cut-away at the rear to improve the departure

angle. Larger-section tyres were used - 7.50x16 rather than the more usual 7.00x16. Both the front and rear axles were reinforced, with the addition of anti-roll bars to improve ride comfort and safety. Series II and IIA-based RAF ambulances were generally fitted with a full-width welded radiator guard.

The interior of the body was changed to accommodate four stretcher patients around 1964 and, by this time, Mickleover Transport, Park Royal Vehicles and Marshalls of Cambridge were building the bodies.

Through all of the chassis changes, the design of the ambulance body remained virtually unchanged until the introduction of the Defender 130 ambulance and the subsequent Wolf XD-130 in 1997.

Army field ambulances

Whilst RAF casualties rode in comparative comfort from 1956, it was not until around 1958 that the Army took delivery of the first of a batch of front-line two-stretcher ambulances, very similar in appearance to the RAF mountain

rescue vehicles and mirroring the sequence of chassis and body changes.

In all, more than 3,000 ambulances were eventually constructed on the Series I, II, and IIA chassis before the design was superseded by the 1-tonne forward-control ambulances which started to enter service during the 1980s.

Similar vehicles were adopted by the Dutch Army, albeit with minor body modifications, and based on diesel-engined Series III chassis.

Top: The addition of Makrolon composite armour indicates that this Series II-based ambulance served in Northern Ireland. *(PW)*

Above: A standard Series II-based ambulance. *(PW)*

101 forward-control ambulance

Constructed on a standard '101' forward-control chassis, this battlefield ambulance was developed according to GSR 3525/1.

The body was large, box-shaped and insulated, being built by Marshalls of Cambridge, this time integral with the cab. Twin rear doors and a fold-down step provided easy access. The body was capable of accommodating two or four stretcher cases, one or two stretcher cases plus four seated or eight seated casualties. Interior ventilation and heating facilities were provided. An oxygen supply was fitted in the rear. The vehicle was equipped with a higher output alternator and a split charging system.

Ambulances intended for the RAF crash-rescue role also included engine pre-heating facility, a trickle charger and radio installation. These vehicles were also equipped with stowage facilities for oxygen/nitrous oxide gas cylinders.

The ambulances remained in service until the late 1990s when they were replaced by the Defender XD-130.

Defender 110 and 130 ambulances

The Land Rover 110 and 127 (the latter subsequently renamed 130) were introduced for military service in the mid-1980s, both lending themselves to the ambulance role although, with the additional length, the 130 was more generally favoured. By this time, Land Rover was also stating that mobile clinics, vaccination units and other medical facilities could be constructed on these chassis.

However, as part of the 'core military Defender' range, Land Rover offered customers a battlefield ambulance constructed on either chassis using a two-stretcher body provided by either Marshalls of Cambridge, or the Andover-based Locomotors company. The Irish Defence Force procured a small number of Defender 130 ambulances fitted with two-stretcher ambulance bodies constructed by Macclesfield Motor Bodies of Cheshire, so clearly Land Rover was equally happy to supply customers with chassis-cab vehicles, allowing the body to be constructed by a third party.

The standard ambulance body followed the already-established principles, although some early examples appear not to have been provided with the distinctive Luton cab roof; where this feature was provided, a linking door allowed entry to the rear compartment from the cab. Windows were provided on the right-hand side. The body was updated in 1989 when the roof was squared off and the previously-flat header panel above the windscreen was replaced by a more angular design. A large roof rack was frequently fitted.

Land Rovers sales literature of the period suggests that bodies could be constructed for carrying up to six stretcher cases or eight seated casualties with plenty of stowage space for medical equipment. Heating or air conditioning could provided as required.

Small numbers of Defender-based ambulances were purchased by all three of the British services, generally powered by the 3.5-litre V8 petrol engine. In British service, they were effectively superseded by the Wolf Defender XD-130, but continued to be offered to export customers.

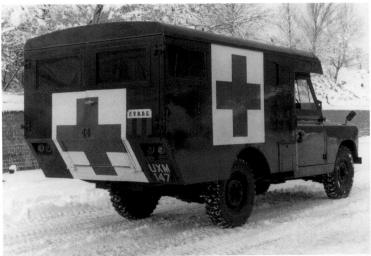

Wolf XD-130 ambulance

Initially code-named 'Pulse', the Marshall-bodied 130in (3.3m) ambulance was always envisaged as one of the standard variants of the Wolf XD range. Although the initial General Statement of Requirements which described the vehicle was not issued until 1991, with the

Above: The oil cooler can be clearly seen on this standard Series II ambulance. The cutaway at the rear enabled the vehicle to negotiate landing-craft ramps. *(PW)*

Above and right:
The standard British ambulance body was fitted to Series I, II and II chassis. *(ST)*

Above: Unusual Lomas coach-built ambulance body on a Series II chassis. *(ST)*

Left: The forward-control 101 was also used as the basis for a standard field ambulance. *(ST)*

Above: Rare picture of the Carter stretcher conversion in action. Troops of the Trucial Oman Scouts carry a casualty from the battlefield to a waiting Westland Whirlwind helicopter, February 1962. *(IWM)*

Right: RAF medical personnel prepare a 'casualty' for evacuation during an excercise in Germany. Note the Lightning F3 fighter in the background. *(RAFM)*

invitations to bid coming a year later, it was envisaged that trials for the vehicle would run alongside the later stages of those for the standard Wolf utility vehicles.

Other contenders for the role included a development of the Iveco 40.10WM and the Pinzgauer, a British-based development of the Austrian Steyr vehicle of this name which dated back to the 1960s. In fact, the Pinzgauer performed so well that it resulted in changes to the MoD's test methods, forcing the designers at both Land Rover and Marshalls, to go back to the drawing board in certain areas. It was only at the conclusion of the trials that the gap between the two vehicles had narrowed sufficiently to keep the Wolf in the running. In terms of 'battlefield mission' performance and 'noise, vibration, harshness' the Steyr emerged as the clear winner.

Land Rover's trump card appeared to be the commonality of components with other vehicles in the fleet, user familiarity, and a five-year vehicle warranty. In January 1996, Land Rover became the supplier of the battlefield ambulance, and Marshalls received a £15 million contract to supply 800 ambualnce bodies for XD-130 chassis. The first vehicles were scheduled to enter service that same year.

The XD-130 ambulance carried a large, box-shaped walk-through body and was fitted to carry four standard NATO stretchers, resuscitation equipment, oxygen bottles and other medical equipment. The stretcher arrangements also allowed the vehicle to carry two stretcher and three seated or six seated casualties.

Land Rover also offered both box shelter and 'pod'-type bodies which could be used to convert a long-wheelbase open vehicle into an ambulance.

Above: This removable 'pod' type body can be used to convert a long-wheelbase open vehicle into an ambulance. *(TM)*

3.3 Fire Appliances

Although it did not go on sale until 1952, the first Land Rover fire appliance was constructed on one of the pre-production 80in (2.03m) chassis. It was a modest machine such as might be useful in a factory or, for example, a power station or woodland estate.

More specialist machines quickly superseded the Rover-supplied equipment, but nevertheless the Land Rover remained a popular basis for conversion into a fire appliance.

As the numbers of Land Rovers in military service grew, it must have been obvious that the vehicle's off-road performance made it eminently suitable for many military fire-fighting duties, including fire-crash-rescue and the more usual fire-fighting duties.

Fire-crash-rescue

Most numerous amongst these were vehicles designed for airfield fire-crash-rescue duties, examples of which the RAF started to receive around 1960.

The vehicle chosen for modification to the role was the, then-current production, Rover 7 (FV18041) - in other words, the 109in (2.77m) Series II pick-up. Designated FV18047, and described as 'truck, fire fighting, airfield crash and rescue', the vehicle was designed to meet Air Ministry requirements for providing rapid intervention rescue facilities for crashed aircraft, and to deal with aircraft brake fires. It was not intended to travel far and would generally only have been used for fire-fighting within, or close to, an airfield perimeter but, both road speed and off-road performance were important assets in this role.

The basic parameters for the vehicle were laid down in Air Ministry Operational Requirement 6231, and the development work was undertaken by the Fighting Vehicles Research & Development Executive (FVRDE) working with SERV RD6 of the Air Ministry. Whilst FVRDE was responsible for the modifications required to the basic vehicle, the Air Ministry took responsibility for specifying the fire-fighting equipment. The specialised equipment was supplied and installed by the Feltham-based company Foamite Limited.

For dealing with various types of fire the vehicle carried two high-pressure foam extinguishers with rubber-covered hoses and a monitor gun; the hoses were coiled and stowed on a frame carried across the rear of the body. Portable water and carbon-dioxide fire extinguishers were also carried in the rear of the vehicle, and small Pyrene-type extinguishers were clipped to the tops of the front wings. Asbestos blankets were also carried.

Two portable air bottles were carried in a light tubular frame fitted at the nearside rear of the vehicle. Rotary air saws and other small rescue tools were stowed in a tool box and three stowage lockers installed in the sides of the rear body. Powerful searchlights were mounted on the cab roof, also an extending site-illuminating lamp. A two-section aluminium extending ladder was supported on the cab and rear of the vehicle. A radio telephone was installed between the two seats.

At the front, a welded brush guard was fitted ahead to protect the radiator and lamps and a good old-fashioned fire-bell was fitted to the bumper apron, alongside a powerful spot lamp. A revolving beacon was frequently fitted on the offside front wing. Clips were fitted to the front wings to retain the doors in the fully-open position. No tailgate or rear tilt were fitted, and the spare wheel was removed from the normal position on the bonnet top. The towing pintle was of the fixed jaw type, with a simple pin, rather than the more familiar hook, for the trailer eye. Lifting/lashing rings were fitted front and rear.

The chassis included all of the modifications which were found on the standard military Land Rover. For example, the suspension was reinforced to provide a better ride and improved handling, an oil cooler was fitted, as was an eight-bladed cooling fan. The front bumper was replaced by the standard type heavy-duty military pattern. The standard

Above: A small fire appliance was offered as a standard factory variant from early in the life of the Series I. *(TM)*

Right: FV18047 was described as 'truck, fire fighting, airfield crash and rescue', and was intended to meet Air Ministry requirements for providing rapid intervention rescue facilities for crashed aircraft and to deal with fires in aircraft brakes. A considerable amount of equipment was carried, including ladders, cutting gear and at least two types of fire extinguisher. *(TM)*

Left and below: The so-called TACR-1 was a Series III based fire-crash-rescue vehicle which started to appear in the early 1970s. Fitted with a purpose-built aluminium body constructed and equipped by HCB-Angus, it was described as 'tactical airfield crash rescue' or 'truck, aircraft, crash rescue'. *(RA)*

military 7.50x16 cross-country tyres were used, but the pressures were adjusted to give 18% deflection under the increased weight of the equipment. The standard 12V electrical system was retained.

The only modification made to the two-man cab was the inclusion of a double-skinned roof panel, into which was installed a hinged circular hatch to provide access to the searchlight.

A brand-new 1960-built Rover 7 was supplied to Foamite in order that the company could produce a prototype. The finished vehicle was put through FVRDE's standard automotive trials on the various test courses to check over-all reliability, and to ensure that the equipment and its mountings had no adverse effect on the structure of the vehicle or handling characteristics.

At the conclusion of these trials, the FVRDE report stated that the 5,796lb (2,629kg) laden weight of the completed vehicle (compared to around 3,600lb (1,633kg) for the unmodified vehicle) was within the specified limits and that the side-overturn angles were satisfactory and there were 'no adverse handling characteristics'. On the test track the vehicle was able to attain a straight-line speed of 60mph (96.5kph),

albeit at the expense of fuel consumption which was down to 14mpg (5km/l)... however, the maximum speed was reduced to 35mph (56kph) on the 'snake' road. On the suspension, rough road and cross-country courses, the handling and control of the vehicle was said to be 'good' although the internal springing of the driver's seat was criticised for being 'too lively' - on production models, a 'Dunlopillo' cushion was fitted, which it was said would allow the

Right: Aircraft crashes inevitably require both rescue and fire-fighting facilities. Here, a Series III military police vehicle heads up a column which also includes a 'lightweight' and a pair of long-wheelbase rescue vehicles. *(RAFM)*

Above: Civilian Series IIB forward-control chassis used as the basis for an RAF airfield fire-crash-rescue truck, almost certainly constructed by HCB-Angus. *(RA)*

driver to adopt a 'more relaxed posture when driving over rough terrain'.

Subject to a number of defects being corrected, the vehicle was accepted for service and an unknown number started to enter service during 1960. The vehicle type was displayed at the FVRDE exhibitions held at Chertsey in 1962, 1966, 1971 and 1981, where the intention was to secure export sales.

When the Series II was superseded in 1961, the same equipment was installed on the Series IIA Rover 9 chassis but, within a decade or so, the vehicle was almost certainly considered obsolete and was replaced by the TACR-1.

TACR-1

By the time the Series IIA was superseded, the original fire-crash-rescue vehicle was starting to look outdated, and the Air Ministry took the opportunity to take a fresh look at the design.

Series III based fire-crash-rescue vehicles, which started to appear in the early 1970s, were fitted with a more-sophisticated purpose-built aluminium body constructed and equipped by HCB-Angus and were described as TACR - 'tactical airfield crash rescue' or 'truck, aircraft, crash rescue' according to which source you refer - later to be re-designated TACR-1 when the Range Rover based TARC-2 was introduced.

The vehicle is easily identified by virtue of the over-sized wheels and tyres, full-width brush guard, bonnet-mounted spare wheel, double front bumpers, and distinctive angular rear wheel arches. Roller-type shutters were used on the rear-facing equipment lockers and extinguishers and pumping equipment was carried inside the body; there was a 100 gallon (454 litre) 'first-aid' water tank. A large square hatch was fitted into the cab roof to allow a crew member to tackle a fire from an elevated position at a safe distance, and an extending aluminium ladder was carried on the right-hand side.

Despite the updating of the vehicle's appearance and equipment, the concept was little changed from the 1960s and the TACR

Left and below:
TACR-1 is easily identified by its, over-sized wheels and tyres, full-width brush guard, bonnet-mounted spare wheel, double front bumpers and distinctive angular rear wheel arches. Pumping equipment was carried inside the body, and there was a 100-gallon (454 litre) 'first-aid' water tank. *(BM)*

Left: Stripped to the minimum to allow the mounting of pumping equipment, this long-wheelbase Series III is towing a powered-axle foam-producing trailer. *(RAFM)*

vehicles were expected to act as rapid intervention fire appliances, particularly at Harrier squadrons, where hopefully the rescue crew would be able to fight a fire sufficiently to evacuate the aircrew, before leaving the larger fire appliances to finish the job.

Similar vehicles were also supplied to the Royal Navy for use at naval air stations.

Domestic fire appliances

Around 1962, the Carmichael company used a 109in (2.77m) chassis to construct a compact, manoeuvrable forward-control domestic fire appliance for use 'at home and overseas, and for operation over narrow roads, steep gradients, and acute bends'. A number of these were supplied to the Army where, despite the forward-control configuration, they were confusingly designated Rover 9.

The vehicle was almost certainly not constructed on the standard Land Rover forward-control chassis and, although the wheelbase remained at 109in (2.77m), the chassis was said to have been extended to provide the forward-control layout. The forward portion of the body, which looked like no other Land Rover, consisted of a driving and crew compartment, while the rear section housed a main pump (capable of delivering 300/350 gallons (1,364/1,511 litre) of water per minute) a 40 gallon (182 litre) water tank, hose reel and suction hoses. A 35ft (10.7m) extending ladder was carried on the roof and there were side lockers for all necessary tools and equipment.

Additional cooling facilities were provided to prevent the engine from overheating during stationary pumping operations, there was also an oil cooler. The engine was fitted with an immersion heater to ensure rapid starting and effective lubrication from cold.

A similar vehicle was constructed for the British Army by HCB-Angus on a standard 110in (2.79m) forward-control chassis.

Other fire appliances

The Australian Army has also used Land Rover fire appliances in both the domestic and fire-crash-rescue roles, in the latter case using a 'drop-in' pod-type fire-fighting body.

Left: Curious-looking Series II based forward-control fire appliance with body and equipment by Carmichael. Dating from the late-1960s, the vehicle ws described as a 3/4 ton Rover 9. *(RA)*

3.4 | Amphibians

It is often said that an army fights the next war with the weapons of the last. Should a third world war have occurred, it was assumed that the attack would have come from the east where the German plains are criss-crossed by rivers.

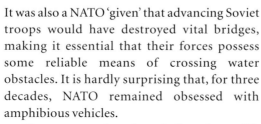

It was also a NATO 'given' that advancing Soviet troops would have destroyed vital bridges, making it essential that their forces possess some reliable means of crossing water obstacles. It is hardly surprising that, for three decades, NATO remained obsessed with amphibious vehicles.

These were the days before heavy-lift helicopters. Without bridges, there were two ways for a military vehicle to cross water, either by 'swimming' or floating across, or by 'wading' or 'fording', with the vehicle driving on the bottom.

Since the Land Rover was likely to be involved in operations virtually anywhere in the world, a technique was required which would allow the vehicle to take to water. One experiment, which was carried out with some success, was to wrap the vehicle in a tarpaulin, and to float it across a river, pulling it from one side to the other using a rope. Although this might have been successful as a field expedient, it was not practicable for large numbers of vehicles, much less a complete

invasion force, and clearly, some other method of flotation was required.

APGP 'Scheme A'

During the late 1950s, the Fighting Vehicles Research and Development Establishment (FVRDE) carried out trials of vehicles fitted with rubber buoyancy bags inflated by the engine exhaust. One such trial mounted a Land Rover on a steel frame inside an oval rubber pontoon... until someone decided it might be better to attach the buoyancy aids to the vehicle, rather than the other way round.

By the early 1960s, the need for an air-portable amphibious vehicle led to the development of a hybrid Series II, described as 'FV18051, truck, airportable, general purpose (APGP)', which employed this technique to make the vehicle float.

The 'military characteristics' of the vehicle were described in a document dated June 1962,

Above and left:
This Series I Land Rover is about to be floated across a river by the simple expedient of wrapping the vehicle up in a large tarpaulin and pushing it across. *(PW)*

stating that a 'requirement exists for a vehicle which can be carried in transport aircraft in numbers which make the fullest use of the payload of the aircraft... this vehicle must fulfill most of the vehicle roles until the arrival of the sea tail and must enable combat and support units to move freely across country and water obstacles with only limited engineer support'. No British vehicle met all these requirements, and the document went on to say that 'a new special truck is required'.

The vehicle was to be both 'simple and robust', with the minimum practical kerb weight, and a payload-to-weight ratio exceeding existing vehicles. Cross-country performance was to be 'better than existing GS vehicles in the equivalent range'. The vehicle was to be capable of floating, fully-laden on inland waters, probably by means of an appliqué flotation kit, which 'need not be stowed on the vehicle but must be capable of being quickly fitted by the driver and one passenger'. When the flotation kit was not fitted,

the approach and departure angles were to be equal to, or better than the existing Series II vehicles and, without the flotation kit, the vehicle was to be capable of negotiating the ramps of aircraft, landing ships, and landing craft 'which were in service from 1965 onwards'.

This was also the time when western armies were excited about multi-fuel engines, power units which would run with almost equal efficiency on diesel, petrol, kerosene, aviation spirit or jet fuel… or for that matter, almost any flammable liquid. The War Office would have been delighted had such a power unit been available, but a petrol engine was said to be acceptable 'as an interim measure'. The operating range, across country, was to be 300 miles (483km) with the multi-fuel engine, or 240 miles (386km) for the petrol engine.

Side-screens and a top were required to protect the crew, and there were to be frames to accept two, or possibly three, stretchers. A hardtop was required to allow the vehicle to be used in the computer, missile and fuze-test roles, and as a communications vehicle; as well as a penthouse tent to allow conversion to the command or office role. As regards weapons, the vehicle was to be capable of carrying the general-purpose machine gun (GPMG), WOMBAT anti-

tank gun, or medium-range anti-tank guided weapon system. Finally, the truck was to be capable of towing a trailer, 105mm Pack howitzer, or other wheeled equipment up to 50% of its gross weight.

As regards air-portability, the 'maximum practical number of vehicles' were to be fitted into an Argosy CC Mk 1, Avro 748 MF, or Beverley aircraft. Stacking of empty vehicles was permitted, but there was to be the minimum of dismantling, since the vehicles were required to be operational 'within one hour of landing'. The fully-loaded vehicle was to be airborne parachute and assault landings capable when carried on a medium stressed parachute platform.

There was never any doubt that the APGP was to be a Land Rover, since the War Office had stated that it was intended to incorporate 'as many standard Land Rover components and assemblies as possible, compatible with fulfilling its operational role'.

Land Rover engineer Mike Broadhead assisted by Norman Busby, produced the design for a heavily modified 109in (2.77m) Series II. Powered by the standard 2,286cc four-cylinder engine, the chassis was fitted with a lower-ratio rear axle and was rated at 1 ton (1,016kg) rather than the normal 3/4 ton

Above and opposite: Dating from around 1962, FV18051 was an attempt at building a Land Rover that was both air-portable and amphibious. The amphibious capability was provided by large buoyancy bags designed to be attached to steel frames and inflated via the engine exhaust. When not in use, both the bags and the frames were carried in underfloor lockers. *(IWM)*

Above and right: Whilst the bags ensured flotation, forward propulsion was provided by the wheels. A small propeller fitted to the propshaft. The vehicle did not enter series production. *(IWM)*

(762kg). Three prototypes were constructed, one of which was shown at the exhibition of military vehicles at Chertsey in 1962.

With a low-sided body, specially-widened aft of the scuttle and shortened at the rear, with no doors or tailgate, it was an odd-looking beast. There were folding seats in the rear, but these do not appear to have been carried across to the production vehicles, which were equipped, instead, with removable squabs and side rails. With the rear seats folded flat, or the side rails removed, the vehicles could be carried, stacked two (or three) high, in a transport aircraft by removing the front wheels of the second vehicle and placing it on top of the first. The two bodies faced in opposite directions, the upper vehicle being held in place by special cradles, with the suspension pulled down to reduce the total height.

There was a high-sided hardtop, consisting of a series of removable flat panels and side curtains, which allowed conversion to the test or communications role. There was also a large penthouse tent, normally carried on the roof, which could be erected to one side to enable the vehicle to be used as a command post or wireless station.

The chassis was filled with foam and the early prototypes were actually able to float unaided... albeit with less than an inch of freeboard. It was obvious that some kind of buoyancy aids were essential and an appliqué flotation kit was developed by RFD Limited, with further developments by Avon Rubber. On the prototypes, the kit consisted of a pair of rubber and canvas oval-shaped buoyancy bags mounted along the sides and rear of the vehicle. These were inflated from the vehicle's exhaust. The bags were carried on removable tubular alloy frames attached to special fittings on the body and chassis. When not in use, they could be deflated, folded away and stowed inside compartments under the rear floor.

Propulsion in the water was provided by the wheels and a small three-bladed propeller on the rear of the propeller shaft; to reduce drag on the road, the propeller could be removed

and replaced by a spacer. Unfortunately, the propeller did not produce sufficient thrust due to the proximity of the differential and, by all accounts, performance in the water was very poor, with a top speed of less than 1.5mph (2.4kph). A rudder was not fitted.

With the initial trials over, the Ministry of Supply issued a contract on 7 June 1962 for 12 vehicles. The contract was extended in October 1964 to cover another eight, this time fitted with winches. Land Rover records suggest that 28 vehicles were actually built although only 20 entered military service.

By the time the vehicle entered production, the Series IIA had completely replaced the Series II, and this was used as the basis for constructing the production vehicles. However, the major change was to the flotation bags which were now being produced by Avon Rubber, reputedly at lower cost, and which were supported on curved, rather than straight, arms. Some photographs show the vehicles to be fitted with four bags, at the front and rear and along each side, others show just three

bags, only at the sides and rear. In some cases, the bags are round, others are oval.

Other changes include the use of the standard military double-height 'pusher' bumpers at front and rear, and the eventual removal of the step rails which had formed simple sills on the prototype.

The vehicles were issued for troop trials between 1963 and 1964, but the type was never adopted or produced in great quantity, effectively being superseded by the 'lightweight' in 1968.

APGP 'Scheme B'

Although it never proceeded beyond the mock-up stage, there was also a second such amphibious Land Rover... 'truck, airportable, general purpose (APGP), scheme B, FV18061'.

This machine employed standard Series II automotive components, with the same transfer case as that used on the APGP 'Scheme A', assembled onto an exoskeleton foam-reinforced plastic body with load-bearing steel inserts. At 97in (2.46m), the wheelbase was

decidedly non-standard, but the unladen weight was reduced to an admirable 3,500lb (1,588kg) which was little more than a standard short-wheelbase Series II.

An artist's impression was included in the 1962 FVRDE exhibition catalogue, showing a sleek, futuristic forward-control vehicle. By the time this had been translated into an engineering model the following year, it looked rather more like an electric milk float. It was subsequently demonstrated at FVRDE, but nothing further came of the project.

Australian military amphibian

Although there is no suggestion that it was related to FV18061, an experimental amphibious vehicle produced for the Australian Army borrowed the curious 97in (2.46m) wheelbase dimension.

Identified by the Australian Army as 'OTAL' (one ton amphibious Land Rover), the vehicle was assembled in late 1965 using as many standard Land Rover components as possible and powered by the 2.6 litre six-cylinder petrol engine.

The body was high-waisted to provide the maximum freeboard and was made up of an engine compartment attached to a pair of separate watertight aluminium sponsons. The first of these was designed to house the driver and two passengers with access provided by shallow drop-down doors, whilst the rear unit provided a cargo area. The front wings were foam-filled to act as buoyancy tanks and closed-cell polyurethane foam was also used to fill the chassis sections and under-floor area.

The engine and transmission were waterproofed and all of the vents and breathers were placed well above the waterline; a short snorkel protruded through the bonnet on the right-hand side and the exhaust pipe was extended to roof level. A mechanical winch was carried on the front apron.

Trials were carried out in February 1966, with cross-country performance described as being 'up to normal Land Rover standards'. In the water it was a different matter. Initially, a propeller was

Right: This view of
FV18051 shows the
side benches which
covered the stowage
lockers for the
flotation equipment.
(TM)

not fitted, the wheels providing the sole means of drive when afloat. Subsequently, some form of 'deflector' was fitted at, or near, each wheel station, which was said to allow the vehicle 'to cope with most inland water flows'.

Despite being demonstrated to the Australian Army, there were no orders forthcoming and the lone prototype was shipped back to the UK, where it remained at Land Rover's off-road testing centre.

Wading

On 6 June 1944, some 37,000 vehicles were landed on the Normandy beaches and, although landing craft carried the vehicles close to the beaches, all had to be waterproofed to allow them to be driven off a ramp and up the beach. An enormous amount of work was required to make this possible, and it is testament to both the methodology, and the care with which the work was carried out, that only around 1% of vehicles were lost.

Wading is fraught with difficulties. If water enters the intake system, the resulting hydraulic lock will destroy the engine. A small amount of water in the ignition system will short-circuit the plugs, whilst water in the fuel system will block the carburettor jets. If the engine stalls with the tail pipe under water, the exhaust system will fill, and the engine cannot be restarted. Water entering junction boxes, lights and instruments will cause short circuits and corrosion leading to unreliability. And water in the axles, transmission and engine lubrication system will cause damage to bearing surfaces which may result in seizure.

During the 1950s, the Amphibious Trials and Training Unit (ATTU) at Instow, North Devon, worked in conjunction with the Fighting Vehicles Research & Development Establishment (FVRDE) at Chertsey, to develop a waterproofing system for all military vehicles which employed various methods of sealing joints and surfaces against water ingress. Bostik adhesive was used to stick

waterproofing fabric to metal surfaces. A self-adhesive plastic sealing tape called Prestikon was used to close small openings and joints. Canvas covers were provided to enclose larger components such as the starter motor, coil, distributor and fuel pump. A silicone compound was used to seal junction boxes and fuses. Purpose-made adapters raised the air-intake inlet above the water line. Finally, surfaces which were vulnerable, rather than vital, were liberally smeared with waterproof grease to prevent corrosion.

A 120-page, War Office document described the 25 man-hours' work required to waterproof a Series I ready for wading to a depth of 60in (1.5m). And, never afraid to state the obvious, the document explained that the last stage of the work was to 'memorise the tasks... which must be done (immediately) after landing... and place this instruction in the PVC bag provided and seal with adhesive tape'. There was an equally long list of work to be completed once the wading was over, and

before the vehicle was considered fit for further service.

Waterproofed vehicles were trialled by immersion. At Chertsey, a vehicle was required to make a series of runs through a deep-water tank followed by 15-minutes static immersion at a depth of 48in (1.22m) with the engine running at full revs before driving out. The final trial was carried out in sea at Instow: the vehicle was disembarked from a landing craft, spending 15 minutes in the sea under its own power, followed by a 10 mile (16km) road run. The engine, axles and transmission were then stripped and examined for water contamination.

Until the appearance of the Royal Marines' Defender XD, no Land Rovers were supplied from the factory prepared for wading. Nevertheless, the ability to disembark from landing craft remains a standard military requirement and a variation of these complex procedures was equally applicable to Series II and III and to the core military Defender.

Above: Partially-stripped 'lightweight', equipped with a makeshift snorkel for deep-water wading. *(PW)*

Above: Not much is known about this amphibious 'light-weight' which was trialled in the late 1960s. Glassfibre floats have been attached to the body sides and at the front. Propulsion in the water was provided by a Dowty Hydrojet unit. *(PW)*

Right: Deep-water wading requires that the vehicle be fitted with a snorkel, and often an exhaust pipe extension. It is also necessary that the electrical equipment is waterproofed. *(PW)*

Above and left: Just one prototype of the FV18061 amphibian was constructed. Whilst the artist's impression showed a sleek, futuristic machine, the reality was rather closer in appearance to a milk float. The vehicle used an exoskeleton foam-reinforced plastic body with load-bearing steel inserts. *(TM [top] PW [left])*

3.5 Gun Ships and Missile Launchers

It is impossible to tell the story of the Land Rover without occasional reference to the Jeep. Just as this vehicle had served as a mount for machine guns and anti-tank weapons during World War Two, so the Land Rover proved to be adaptable to a similar role. By the time the Defender came on the scene, the Land Rover had been used to mount anti-aircraft and anti-tank guided weapons as well as the more usual machine guns.

Historically, the Army tended to carry out their own modifications to produce a weapons platform, either using Army workshop units or subcontracting the work to a specialised company, and only with the introduction of the Defender have such variants been available direct from the factory.

M40 106mm recoilless rifle

In World War Two the US Army started to fit recoilless anti-tank rifles to Jeeps. The lightweight, compact size and manoeuvrability of the vehicle meant that it was often able to sneak up to an advantageous firing position and take a shot at a less manoeuverable armoured fighting vehicle. It also presented a relatively small target and was generally able to make a quick getaway.

The weapon of choice at this time was the recoilless rifle, a large-calibre weapon designed so that recoil forces are cancelled out by sending

thrust backwards to counter that which goes forward when the projectile is fired. Very little stress is transferred to the weapon mount or to the ground, but the disadvantage is that the flashback of flame and smoke is easily spotted.

By 1955, the US military forces were using the 106mm M40, with high-explosive anti-tank (HEAT), high-explosive squash-head (HESH), high-explosive plastic-tracer (HEP-T), and anti-personnel rounds (APERS-T). The weapon incorporated an M8C spotting rifle co-axially mounted above the barrel, allowing the gunner to check his aim and trajectory before firing an expensive anti-tank round; in later guns, a laser sighting device was used for the same purpose. According to the type of projectile chosen, the weapon was able to penetrate 5.9in (150mm) of armour at a 60° impact angle at up to 1,200 yards (1,097m).

The weapon saw extensive service during the Korean War and later in Vietnam. It has also equipped forces in Europe, as well as with

Above and left:
Saudi Arabia bought
a number of
these Series II
'lightweights'
equipped with the
M40 106mm
recoilless rifle.
The conversion
work was carried
out by Marshalls
of Cambridge but
the vehicle was
marketed by
Land Rover. *(PW)*

literally dozens of nations around the world. British Army M40s were replaced by the MOBAT and WOMBAT guns, but overseas it was a different matter. In November 1976, Marshalls of Cambridge came up with an M40A1 conversion of the 'lightweight' for the Saudi-Arabian Government. Approximately 100 vehicles were converted, with the first entering service in 1977. Some saw service in the first Gulf War, being used to particularly good effect with the Saudi Arabian National Guard.

Although the conversion work was carried out by Marshalls, Rover marketed the vehicle direct to foreign governments.

The vehicle was supplied with the M40A1 rifle, almost certainly supplied by Pakistan Machine Tool Factory Limited, together with the standard M79 tripod mount, giving a 180° arc of fire forwards when fitted in the vehicle, but remaining easily dismountable for firing in a ground position. Rover claimed that the vehicle retained all of the mobility of the standard 'lightweight' and was able to quickly assume a strategic position and fire the gun before moving on to another location.

The standard windscreen was replaced by a unique split screen, constructed from square, tubular sections. This allowed the gun barrel to be traversed over the bonnet and clamped in the travelling position. Other modifications included side-facing drop-down seats in the rear and an additional under-seat fuel tank to compensate for increased fuel consumption. Ammunition stowage lockers/bins and blast shields to protect the wings, bonnet and spare wheel when firing forwards were fitted. The vehicle was carried on 7.50x16 tyres. No hood was fitted since there was no frame and no satisfactory means of attaching it to the body. Some versions were constructed without the bonnet-mounted spare wheel in an effort to improve visibility.

A similar specification is currently offered on the Defender 90.

The modification was actually more common on a standard long-wheelbase chassis - the Australians being particularly keen on this configuration - but both the British and Spanish Armies also mounted the M40 gun onto standard 88in (2.24m) Series I and II chassis; the Spanish favouring the Santana Model 88 Militar.

Above and right:
As the name suggests, the recoilless rifle generates very little recoil when fired, which makes it ideal for mounting on a small vehicle, producing a fast, agile tank buster. The tripod mount allows the weapon to be fired from inside the vehicle or removed for ground firing. *(ST [top] PW [right])*

The Dutch Marines used 88in (2.24m) 'lightweights' without body modifications, although the tailgate was removed.

MOBAT and WOMBAT anti-tank guns

The US was not the only country developing anti-tank weapons and in the late 1940s, the Royal Ordnance Factory, Woolwich, London began work on the Battalion Anti-Tank gun, or BAT.

The BAT was the first recoilless rifle system issued to postwar British Army infantry units at battalion level. Proving to be somewhat too large, it was replaced by the lighter MOBAT in 1959. During the early 1960s, MOBAT was succeeded by the longer-range, lightweight WOMBAT which had been developed by the Royal Armaments Research & Development Establishment (RARDE) at Fort Halstead, Sevenoaks, Kent.

All three generations of these anti-tank weapons employed the same type of 120mm L1 (HESH) ammunition. Rather than relying on

weight and velocity to penetrate armour, the squash head flattens out against the target, generating a stream of molten metal and causing internal spalling. By the time WOMBAT was introduced, the L1 round was effective against a static target at a range of about 1,000yds (1,097m) and against moving targets at 800yds (732m); the armour penetration performance

Top and above: The Defender 90 was also used as a platform for the M40 106mm recoilless rifle. *(TM)*

141

Above and right:
Both long- and short-wheelbase Series IIs were used as a 'portee' for the M40. *(RA)*

Left: The British equivalent of the US Army's M40 was WOMBAT, a light recoilless rifle suitable for vehicle mounting. *(RA)*

Left: Swingfire was a hard-hitting, anti-tank missile using a high-explosive (HE) hollow-charge warhead. The weapon could easily be mounted on a variety of vehicles, such as the Series II Land Rover. *(TM)*

Above: The Swingfire missile installation in a long-wheelbase Series II. *(TM)*

was never revealed. As with the M40 recoilless rifle, there was also a co-axial spotting rifle; for BAT and MOBAT, this was a modified .303in Bren gun but by the time WOMBAT was introduced, the 12.7mm L40A1 gun was employed.

Both BAT and MOBAT were mounted on a two-wheeled carriage, and were designed to be towed, muzzle first, behind, for example, a Land Rover or Champ.

In an attempt to reduce weight to the minimum, WOMBAT used lightweight alloys wherever possible as well as eliminating all unnecessary components and equipment, bringing the weight down to around 650lb (295kg), compared to 1,650lb (748kg) of the MOBAT. One factor in the weight reduction was the elimination of the standard towed carriage in favour of what was little more than a braced post-type mount on a lightweight close-spaced axle assembly. Without any provision for towing, the wheeled chassis of the WOMBAT simply allowed the gun to be manoeuvred into a firing position. For transport, it was necessary to use a gun 'portee'.

The vehicle initially chosen as a 'portee' for the WOMBAT in 1960, was the short-wheelbase Series II, and the so-called 'WOMBAT kit' carried the weapon in a cradle clamp mounted in the rear compartment. Loading was effected using a small hand-operated winch via a lightweight ramp which hooked over the base of the tailgate. When the gun was loaded and secured in the travelling position, the mount was positioned more-or-less over the centre-line of the rear axle, but the length of the barrel was such that some 2-3ft (61-91cm) protruded at the rear and a similar amount extended over the bonnet. This meant that it was impossible to fit a windscreen. The barrel was secured by a clamp carried on a tubular frame attached to the windscreen pivots. The rear bulkhead was cut away and the rear inner wings were modified to accommodate stowage tubes for carrying spare rounds. There was no top or sidescreens fitted to the vehicle. The spare wheel was carried on the bonnet.

WOMBAT was a large piece of equipment and, when loaded onto the Land Rover, left little

room for the usual three-man gun crew, which almost certainly meant that two Land Rovers were required to make up an operational WOMBAT team.

The gun was normally fired from a dug-in position, but in an emergency, could be fired without dismounting it from the vehicle, although it was recommended that it be aimed at right angles to the chassis centreline.

Whether or not this was actually possible with the 88in (2.24m) chassis is hard to say but it must have quickly become obvious that the installation was far from satisfactory and attention was turned to adapting the 109in (2.77m) Series II... although it has to be pointed out that the Royal Marines successfully deployed WOMBAT mounted in the rear of the 88in (2.24m) 'lightweight' with a tubular steel framework fitted across the bulkhead in place of the windscreen to support the barrel during transit.

With the 109in (2.77m) chassis, the gun was still loaded into the rear compartment using the winch, and ramp. The barrel was secured in the same type of cradle. The centre of the gun

mount was fitted further back, behind the rear axle, and whilst 2-3ft (61-91cm) still protruded behind the vehicle. At least there was room for a windscreen, albeit adapted to remain almost vertical. Again, no top or side screens were fitted, but there was room for the ramp to be carried inside the body.

The larger vehicle also provided sufficient space for a driver and the three-man crew, one

Above: The prototype forward-control '101' mounting an array of six Swingfire missiles in what was known as the Beeswing mount. *(TM)*

Above: Rear view of the Beeswing installation showing the three pairs of Swingfire missiles on the Y-shaped launch assembly. *(TM)*

occupying the passenger seat, one sitting on the rear nearside inner wing, forward of the gun mount, and one on the rear offside inner wing behind the gun mount. There were also stowage racks for six extra rounds behind the front seats, with additional ammunition carried in a trailer.

In this form WOMBAT entered British Army service in 1962, intended to be used by both infantry and airborne units, as the 'recoilless anti-tank gun truck mount, FV18045', albeit the Series II had, by then, been replaced by the Series IIA.

WOMBAT's last operational use was in the Falklands in 1981, but it was already obsolete by that time and replacement by the wire-guided and far more accurate MILAN anti-tank missile had begun in the late 1970s.

TOW

The Danish Armed Forces adapted some 88in (2.24m) 'lightweights' to mount the US-manufactured BGM-71A TOW (tube launched, optically tracked, wire guided) anti-tank missile.

Designed in the mid-1960s by the Hughes Aircraft Corporation to replace the 106mm recoilless rifle, TOW missiles were frequently fitted to helicopters in service in Vietnam. The missile was fitted with a shaped charge and had an effective range of 200-10,000yds (183-9,144m). The weapon was fired from a substantial post-type mounting in the rear of the Land Rover; a small saddle on the mounting provided a seat for the gunner.

Vigilant anti-tank missiles

The Germans had experimented with wire-guided anti-tank missiles during World War Two, but the idea of creating a fast, mobile tank-buster by mounting such missiles onto a wheeled vehicle almost certainly dates back to the mid-1950s. Two Australian-built Malkara wire-guided anti-tank missiles were placed on a

hydraulic launch arm fitted to a modified Humber 'Pig'.

In the UK, Malkara was followed by the experimental Orange William missile which, in the early 1960s, was superseded by the originally Vickers-designed Vigilant. Eventually produced by the British Aircraft Corporation (BAC), Vigilant was the first reliable British wire-guided anti-tank missile. The weapon was a lightweight man-portable unit with a range of 1,500yds (1,372m). The shaped-charge warhead was capable of penetrating the armour of most main battle tanks of the period. The missile was fired remotely using a combined sight/controller on a separation cable, the missile being guided onto the target by signals fed through a cable in response to movements of the joystick control by the gunner.

From around 1963, Vigilants had been turret mounted in pairs on Ferret reconnaissance vehicles making an excellent 'shoot and scoot' weapon. At the 1966 exhibition of military vehicles held at Chertsey, a long-wheelbase Series II was demonstrated with a pair of Vigilants on a traversable tubular-steel launcher mounted in the cargo area. Three more missiles were carried on the launcher frame and it was claimed that there was space for carrying more missiles behind the centre bulkhead. Designated 'truck, general service, guided weapon', it was claimed that minimal modification was required to prepare the vehicle for the missile installation.

Swingfire anti-tank missiles

In the mid-1960s, Vigilant was replaced by Swingfire, a new, hard-hitting, anti-tank missile which, compared to its predecessors, was a quantum leap forward. Swingfire quickly proved to be both a reliable and accurate missile.

The rocket motor could be vectored to allow control at lower speeds than were normally achievable by aerodynamic control. It was also possible to separate the launch vehicle and

Above: A Defender 90 mounting the MILAN anti-tank missile system; four missiles were carried in the stowage tubes fiited across the back of the vehicle. *(PW)*

Above: British troops excercise in a MILAN-equipped Wolf Defender rapid deployment vehicle. *(BM)*

sighting equipment. This combined with the use of an electronic 'gathering programme', meant that it was no longer necessary for the gunner to fire the missile directly at the target, allowing the launch position to remain hidden. Providing the target could be seen in the sights, the 'gathering programme' brought the missile into the operator's field of view after launch, when it would be guided onto the target by joystick control.

Swingfire carried a 15.4lb (7kg) hollow charge of high-explosive and offered an effective range of 150-4,500yds (137-4,115m), with a flight time of 26 seconds to the maximum range. Although it was said to be very accurate, a degree of skill was still required on the part of the operator to 'fly' the missile to the target. Nevertheless, Swingfire was capable of penetrating up to 31.5in (800mm) of armour, making it more than a match for any then current armoured vehicle.

Finally entering British Army service in 1969,

and quickly replacing Vigilant, Swingfire was claimed to be capable of penetrating the armour of the heaviest tanks in the Warsaw Pact armoury.

Beeswing anti-tank missile system

By the end of the 1960s, Land Rover had begun work on what was to become the 101in (2.6m) forward-control gun tractor. During the development period, trials were also conducted with a view to using the 101 as a mount for the Swingfire system for use by infantry units.

Still carrying a trials' registration number, one of the prototypes was delivered to the British Aircraft Corporation where it was trial-fitted with a multi Swingfire system dubbed Beeswing. In what would now be called the TEL role (transporter, erector, launcher), Beeswing was designed to be installed on the rear loadbed of the 101, providing three pairs of missiles arranged in a ready-to-fire configuration. Flanking missiles were orientated at 45 ° from the

Left: MILAN is a second-generation tube-launched spin-stabilised anti-tank guided weapon (ATGW), armed with a sealed 103mm HEAT warhead. The weapon can be launched either from the ground or from the vehicle mount. (PW)

centre unit to give an effective 90^0 coverage without requiring the launcher to be traversered.

The equipment consisted of a tubular Y-shaped launch assembly holding the six missiles at a maximum 10^0 elevation, and a base pallet holding the launch assembly in a ready-to-use position, whilst providing stowage facilities for use during transit. Cables, connectors and a separation sight were stowed in two boxes fixed to the front of the base pallet. The missiles were carried in hermetically-sealed launcher boxes. The system could be broken down into convenient packages allowing transportation by a three-man crew.

All of the necessary electrical connections were made as the missile boxes were loaded into the launch assembly. Once the target was acquired, missiles could be fired at two-second intervals. A pair of reload missiles could also be carried in the centre launcher position giving a total of eight missiles.

With all of the equipment stowed for transport, the vehicle remained suitable for air transport or air-dropping and could be slung under a helicopter if required.

Both vehicle and equipment were tested at the Military Vehicles Experimental Establishment (MVEE), and BAC's publicity material suggested that system had been constructed especially for the British Army. Although trials continued using production 101s, the equipment does not appear to have entered service.

A 'palletised version' of the Swingfire system, suitable for mounting on a Land Rover, was constructed under licence in Egypt. This may have been similar to Beeswing but, by the early 1970s, infantry units had abandoned Swingfire in favour of the smaller and simpler MILAN missile system.

MILAN anti-tank missile

Design work on the MILAN infantry anti-tank missile was started back in the 1960s by the Franco-German Euromissile consortium, a

joint venture between Messerschmidt-Bölkow-
Blohm GmbH and Aerospatiale Matra;
British Aerospace joined in about 1973 to
produce MILANs for the British Army.
The first prototypes appeared in 1969, with the
first production examples being delivered in
1973.

MILAN (*missile d'infanterie léger anti-char*
- infantry light anti-tank missile) is a second-
generation tube-launched spin-stabilised anti-
tank guided weapon (ATGW). MILAN carried
a sealed 103mm HEAT warhead, which was
guided to the target by a 'semi-automatic
command to line of sight' (SACLOS) system
operating via feedback from an infra-red (IR)
tracking module. Designed to be launched
either from the ground or from a vehicle
mount, the weapon had a range of
approximately 2,200yds (2,012m).

The entry into service of the heavily-
armoured T-72 tank with Warsaw Pact forces

almost led to the cancellation of the MILAN
project, but the improved MILAN 2 appeared
in 1984 specifically to deal with this particular
threat. MILAN 2 then entered service with the
French, German and British Armies. In 1993
the tandem-warhead MILAN 2T variant was
announced, designed to defeat explosive
reactive armour (ERA). This used the improved
115mm-calibre warhead of MILAN 2 but
with the addition of a 30mm diameter HE
primary charge mounted in a nose probe.
MILAN 3 was then developed to reduce
susceptibility to electronics jamming systems,
and entered service with the French Army in
1995. MILAN 3 used the tandem-warhead and
an improved guidance system not affected
by decoys.

Operation of the weapon is virtually
foolproof. The missile tube is simply clipped to
the firing post, aimed at a reference point above
the target, using the optical or thermal-

imaging sight, and fired by pressing a button. Initial ejection from the tube is by compressed gas, which means that no specific protection is required to prevent blow-back damage to the vehicle, and there is no distinctive 'firing signature'. Sufficient gas remains to eject the tube from the post ready for the next round to be positioned immediately. It is possible for a well-trained crew to achieve a rate of fire of three rounds a minute.

As soon as the missile is released, the fins open and the main propulsion motor ignites. All the gunner has to do is to keep the crosshairs of the sight on the target; the missile remains connected to the firing module by wire until the moment of impact.

The lightweight of the system, and ease of mounting, maked it easily adaptable to a range of vehicles. The Defender provides a typical vehicle mount and other nations have used similar machines - the French, for example,

have used both the Hotchkiss M201 and the Peugeot P4, whilst the Belgian Army have fitted the system to the Minerva Land Rover. The standard catalogue version offered by Land Rover is the Defender 110, but MILAN has also been mounted on the Defender 90 and the Defender 130 pick-up, as well as on the Defender 90 MRCV chassis.

As installed in the vehicle, the MILAN system consists of little more than a firing post bolted into the rear, slightly ahead of the rear axle. Four missiles are carried in sealed transport tubes in a rack across the rear of the vehicle, with the tailgate generally removed, or in a rack against the rear of the front seats; the MRCV carries eight missiles, in two racks, placed on either side of the wider load bed. The height of the post precludes the fitting of a top or frame, but a protective roll bar is fitted across the body behind the front seats.

Above: A Wolf Defender fitted with the British Army's weapons mount installation kit (WMIK). This includes a circular mount for a heavy machine gun. *(BM)*

3.6 High-Mobility and Tracked Vehicles

The Land Rover is rightly famed for excellent off-road performance, but there are times when this is not quite enough and, over the years, there have been attempts to modify the vehicle to provide enhanced performance ranging from the 'on stilts' look of the Cuthbertson through the half-track Centaur to the over-sized Straussler wheels.

None was especially successful but all are equally interesting, and all were tried for possible military application.

Cuthbertson

First appearing in the early 1960s, the Cuthbertson conversion bolted the standard Land Rover chassis to a full-length sub-frame carrying pairs of solid-tyred bogie wheels at each wheel station. The front bogie was provided with steering effort through a hydraulic power-assisted system. The standard wheels were replaced by sprockets driving endless nylon/cotton-reinforced rubber tracks fitted with steel cleats.

By all accounts the conversion, which was carried out by J. A. Cuthbertson & Sons of Biggar, Scotland, provided excellent stability despite the increased height of the vehicle. The weight of the sub-frame and bogies, which put the unladen weight of an 88in (2.24m) Land Rover up to a massive 5,500lb (2,495kg) ensured that the centre of gravity remained low.

The conversion was excellent on soft and marshy ground and the Ministry of Defence thought that the low ground pressure imposed by the tracks would make the vehicle ideal for bomb disposal work. Both Series I and Series II vehicles, in both long and short-wheelbase forms, were converted, and photographs exist of a Series 3 'lightweight', but the numbers involved were relatively small.

Straussler wheels

During the early 1950s, the prolific Austrian inventor Nicholas Straussler had experimented with over-sized high-flotation wheels which allowed a vehicle to cross marshland and shallow water obstacles by making the wheels virtually float on the surface. The special wheels were fitted in place of the standard equipment, and provided propulsion in the water by means of

Above and left:
Ungainly though it might have been in appearance, the Cuthbertson conversion provided enhanced mobility combined with low ground pressure, and was favoured for bomb-disposal work. Series I and II vehicles were converted as well as a small number of 'lightweights'.
(PW [top] TM [left])

bars across the tread face and scoops on the sides. The wheels were trialled on Jeeps, Champs and Land Rovers, but proved a little too unwieldy for field use.

In the early 1970s, further trials were conducted with a Series II fitted with huge low-pressure, slick 'doughnut'-type tyres which, again, provided both buoyancy and propulsion. The vehicle was an extraordinary sight, skimming across the surface of the water, throwing up huge rooster tails from the tyres, but the trials were abandoned and the project never reached fruition.

High-flotation tyres were revived again in the mid-1980s when Gloster Saro modified a 'lightweight', equipping it with over-sized Goodyear Wrangler dumper truck-type tyres for possible use in the Falkland Isles. However, these tyres were more modest affairs intended for use on soft, wet ground and marshland rather than on water.

Roadless

In the late 1950s, Roadless Traction Limited of Hounslow, Middlesex, undertook development work on an interesting conversion to a Series II which had been created by the Forestry Commission. In order to increase the ground clearance and to provide improved traction, the Forestry Commission workshops had fitted the vehicle with 10x28 wheels and tyres on high-clearance axles taken from a Roadless Fordson Major tractor.

The turning circle was extremely poor and the large wheels meant that the gear ratios were all way too high. Although the 10x28 tyres were retained, Roadless removed the axles and replaced them with Studebaker units fitted with Kirkstall planetary hub reduction gears. In order to improve the steering lock, the front axle was 14in (36cm) wider than the rear. Needless to say, some drastic body modifications were required to accommodate the axles and wheels.

Following extensive trials, Rover gave approval to the vehicle which was marketed as the Roadless 109, with either a petrol or diesel engine.

Inevitably, the Fighting Vehicles Research & Development Establishment (FVRDE) were informed of the vehicle and put it through

Both pages: These low-pressure high-flotation wheels allow this Series II to effectively skim across a body of water. The major disadvantage, of course, is that the wheels would not be suitable for road use and would need to be carried inside the vehicle when not in use. *(TM)*

Right: Gloster Saro modified a 'lightweight' in the mid-1980s, equipping it with over-sized Goodyear Wrangler dumper tyres for possible use in the Falklands. *(PW)*

Right: Gloster Saro modified a 'lightweight' in the mid-1980s, equipping it with over-sized Goodyear Wrangler dumper tyres for possible use in the Falklands. *(PW)*

trials at Chertsey. It appears that the military remained unimpressed, perhaps because the truly formidable off-road performance - the vehicle could literally climb up steps - was obtained at the expense of safe driving on road surfaces.

Centaur

Rather more serious, was the Laird Centaur, a half-tracked machine developed as a private venture by Laird (Anglesey) Limited, 'with assistance from Land Rover'. Work started in 1977, with the first prototypes appearing in April 1978, and it was anticipated that series production would begin in 1979.

Laird described the Centaur as a 'multi-purpose military vehicle system', and it was intended to combine the ease of operation of a wheeled vehicle with the performance and off-road capabilities of a tracked vehicle. It was hardly a new idea. Citroën had produced half-tracks in the 1920s using the Kégresse system,

and the German Army produced a whole family of expensive and superbly-engineered half-track vehicles during World War Two. Similarly, the US Army's M3/M5 half-tracks were widely used by the Allies throughout the war and went on to serve with the Israeli Defence Force well into the latter half of the 20th century.

However, by the 1950s, improvements in tyre and transmission technology meant that most military pundits believed the half-track concept was obsolete. Laird, clearly, did not agree and the company's designers attempted to combine elements of existing well-proven vehicles to build a new half-track.

The basis of the vehicle was the long-wheelbase chassis and cab of the Stage One, which was extended by the addition of a rigid steel platform behind the cab. This allowed the rear axle to be removed and replaced by a shortened version of the lightweight track and suspension system from the British Army's CVR(T) (combat vehicle reconnaissance, tracked) family.

Left: In the late 1950s, Roadless Traction fitted over-sized wheels and agricultural tyres to a heavily-modifed Series II in order to increase the ground clearance and to provide improved traction. It was trialled by the Forestry Commission and at FVRDE. *(TM)*

Below: The Centaur was produced by Lairds of Anglesey. The prototype, seen here, used an extended long-wheelbase Stage One carrying a shortened version of the lightweight track and suspension system from the British Army's CVR(T) family. *(TM)*

The engine was the familiar Buick-derived Rover V8 which, for this application, was tuned to produce 156bhp from 3,528cc. When combined with the Range Rover's permanent four-wheel drive system, using a four-speed gearbox and two-speed transfer box, it gave the 3 ton (3,048kg) machine a top speed on the road of 50mph (80.5kph). A lockable centre differential transmitted power equally to the front axle and the track system.

At the front, the standard axle was suspended on multi-leaf elliptical springs and was steered by the standard recirculating-ball system. Although there was no power assistance, steering was the same as that of a conventional wheeled vehicle. No steering action was available from track braking.

At the rear, the weight of the vehicle was carried on three rubber-tyred steel disc road wheels - as compared to the five used on the CVR(T) - independently suspended on torsion bars. The track was driven from the front sprocket and was tensioned by means of a hydraulic ram. A single idler wheel at the rear was fitted, with no track return rollers. Rear braking was by inboard twin calliper discs.

Ground clearance was slightly improved when compared to the standard Land Rover of the period, at 10in (25.4cm). However, the increased weight and width gave the Centaur a very low centre of gravity and, combined with the power of the engine and the traction available, this provided excellent off-road performance.

The cab was more or less of standard appearance, but the rear of the body was approximately 16in (41cm) wider than the front. The doors were angled outwards to accommodate this difference. At the front, the distinctive grille of the Stage One was retained, as were the double-height 'pusher bumpers' as fitted to military Land Rovers.

The manufacturers claimed that the cost of the vehicle compared very favourably to that of a standard Land Rover and that, since the driver's controls were unchanged and the front wheels were still used for steering, driver training issues were minimal. On the

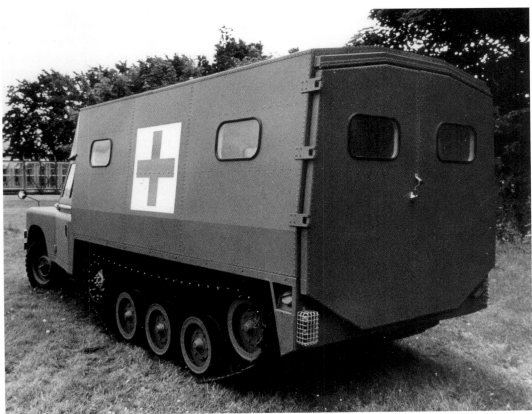

Above and opposite: Lairds belived that the Centaur had a real military future and produced a number of variants for possible consideration by the British Army. One example was shipped to Norway for trials but the only sales went to Oman. *(TM)*

downside, of course, the maintenance requirement was increased and, with only 16.5 gallons (75 litre) of fuel on board, the range for the heavy machine must have been well below 250 miles (402km).

The standard load-carrying variant could accommodate a 3 ton (3,048kg) payload in the 129in (3.3m) long load bed and was provided with a full-length top and side curtains; a full-depth tailgate was fitted at the rear, doubling as a step when lowered. Alternative roles included 10-man personnel carrier, mine layer, recovery vehicle, gun tractor for the Rapier anti-aircraft missile, and gun/missile mount; in the latter role, the Centaur could, typically, be adapted to carry the 106mm recoilless anti-tank gun, Swingfire, MILAN or TOW anti-tank missile system, 20mm anti-aircraft guns, 60mm mortar system or 7.62mm machine guns.

A fully-enclosed vehicle was also constructed. This could be used as a four-stretcher ambulance or communications vehicle. Laird also announced that a fully-armoured variant would be made available which could be adapted to provide a battlefield ambulance, command or reconnaissance vehicle armed with turret-mounted 7.62mm machine guns.

By the early 1980s the vehicle was ready for production. The Stage One was still being used as the basic chassis, and external changes were minimal, with the only noticeable difference being the shape of the door sills, the inclusion of a bonnet mount for the spare wheel, a much reduced depth to the tailgate and improved departure angles by virtue of cutaway rear corners.

Two pre-production models were sold to the Oman Government in 1978, and the British Army shipped one example to Norway for cold-weather trials. Sadly, the British Army did not buy into the concept and, despite a lot of interest from overseas, by 1985 escalating development costs combined with low sales meant that the project was abandoned.

Total production is believed to amount to seven or eight vehicles, at least one of which was based on the later Defender 110.

Above and opposite: Total production of the Centaur is believed to amount to just seven or eight vehicles, most were based on the Stage One, but at least one used the later Defender 110 chassis. *(TM)*

3.7 | Armoured Land Rovers

Various attempts were made during World War Two to produce armoured Jeeps, none of which made it into production, power-to-weight ratio generally proving to be an insurmountable stumbling block. Clearly, there are considerable logistic advantages in being able to deploy a small armoured vehicle which is not only easy to drive, but which shares part inventory and maintenance procedures.

On this basis, an armoured Land Rover would seem to offer a solution to a number of military problems.

The most recent manifestation of the armoured Land Rover is the Defender-based 'snatch' vehicle, which has already been deployed to Iraq. The best known is probably the Shorland, but other examples include the Glover Webb 'armoured patrol vehicle', the Hotspur Armoured Products Limited Dragoon and Sandringham 6, the Skirmisher 4x4 and Hussar 6x6 armoured personnel carriers from Penman Engineering Limited.

Shorland armoured patrol car

Development of the Shorland armoured patrol car began in the early 1960s when the Royal Ulster Constabulary (RUC) was searching for a replacement for the armoured personnel carriers in use at the time. The RUC believed that the Land Rover would provide a suitable basis for a

well-protected law-enforcement vehicle which was not overtly militaristic in appearance.

The first prototype appeared in 1961 having been sketched by Ernie Lustie and constructed around a standard 109in (2.77m) Series II in the Belfast workshops of the Ministry of Home Affairs. Photographs show a slab-sided, boxy vehicle. Although the front wings remained more-or-less standard, the headlamps were moved to a low-down position in the wing fronts to allow the use of an armoured shutter to protect the radiator. The bonnet was also armoured. The doors were replaced by full-length armoured types with small hatches in place of the windows. At the rear, there was a slab-sided, bob-tailed armoured body mounting a small turret which carried a .30 calibre machine gun. A hatch in the rear provided an emergency escape point.

The resulting vehicle was considerably heavier than the standard Land Rover and there was some doubt as to whether the chassis would

Above: This field expedient armoured rail car was developed by the REME workshops in Kenya to provide a guard for trains which were at risk of attack during the emergency there in the early 1950s. *(TM)*

have sufficient strength. In 1963, the prototype was sent to Solihull where Rover's engineers suggested that the chassis, wheels and tyres should be reinforced. By August 1964 the prototype was back in Northern Ireland being demonstrated to the British Army but without success.

Undeterred, the RUC pressed on but, before finalising the design for production, proposed reducing the apparent bulk of the body and, at the same time, improving ballistic performance by increasing the angle of the sloped sides. Following further modifications, a production contract was placed with Short Brothers & Harland Limited and production began at the companys' Newtonards factory in Co Down.

The first examples, based on the 109in (2.77m) Series II, came off the production line in July 1965. Known as the 'Mk 1', these early Shorlands were powered by the 2,286cc four-cylinder engine, and had .30in (7.25mm) thick armoured bodies. The standard chassis was strengthened to support the armoured body, and Aeon hollow-rubber spring assisters were included in the suspension system. The four-wheel-drive system was permanently engaged and the drive-line was upgraded by the use of the heavy-duty ENV axles. The transmission and transfer gearbox from the civilian forward-control model was fitted.

There was a manually-operated turret which was rotatable through 360°. The standard weapon was a .30 calibre Browning with an optical periscope sight, or a 7.62mm general-purpose machine gun (GPMG); smoke dischargers could be fitted to the turret sides. Other weapons could also be mounted and, at the 1966 Farnborough Display, a Shorland was exhibited with turret-mounted Vickers Vigilant anti-tank missiles.

Short Brothers described the vehicle as being 'an armoured body fitted to a slightly-modified long-wheelbase Land Rover chassis', claiming that it had been 'designed to meet a worldwide

Above and right:
This mock-up of the
Shorland armoured
car appeared in
1961 and was
constructed by the
Royal Ulster
Constabulary on a
long-wheelbase
Series II. The turret
was almost certainly
taken from a Ferret
or Saracen
armoured vehicle.
(TM)

requirement for an economical vehicle especially suited to certain types of tasks performed, according to local circumstances, by military, para-military and police forces... including reconnaissance, border patrol, convoy escort, internal security and mobile police duties'. The vehicle's main advantage lay in the fact that it drove, and was maintained, like a standard Land Rover - there was no need to re-train crews or maintenance personnel, and some 80-85% of parts were interchangeable with the standard machine.

The accommodation for a driver, commander and turret gunner in the armoured body was necessarily somewhat cramped. The driver and commander were located in front seats, whilst the gunner was seated centrally behind, and slightly above them with his head in the turret... but, of course, he could also sit on the opened turret door.

Plastic-faced polyurethane foam was applied to the interior of the hull. The floor was of glass-fibre composite material providing some

protection against the IRA's favoured nail and pipe bombs. A hinged armoured screen was provided to protect the laminated-glass windscreen and drop-down visors for the driver and commander. Bullet-proof hatches were installed in the doors. Others for observation and escape were provided in the turret and at the rear; all were seamed and channelled to prevent the ingress of bullet 'splash'. Although the front-end appeared standard, armoured protection was also provided for the engine and radiator. The fuel tank and a spare wheel were contained in a 'bustle' at the rear - an armoured compartment, separated from the crew area.

A fresh-air heating system was installed inside the body. 'High-capacity extraction equipment' could also be provided for use in hot climates.

All of this carried a weight penalty and the kerb weight had increased to more than 6,000lb (2,722kg) which, inevitably, compromised the power-to-weight ratio. Nevertheless, quoted top speed remained in the order of 50mph (80kph)

Above: Production Mk 4 Shorland armoured car on a 109in Series III chassis; there was also an armoured personnel carrier variant on the same chassis. *(TM)*

even if this was at some cost in fuel consumption.
Long-range tanks could be specified, doubling
the fuel load.

Two demonstrator vehicles were trialled by
the General Service Unit of the Kenya Police
Force between January and February 1966 and
the vehicles were reported as having performed
'extremely well' over 1,700 miles (2,736km) of
arduous on and off-road trials.

Deliveries began in the spring of 1966, with
10 vehicles supplied to the RUC; deliveries were
also made to the Bahrain State Police, and a
'para-military force in the Congo'. By 1971,
almost 200 vehicles had been constructed, and
production had been moved to Belfast. As
launched in 1966, the vehicle was priced at
£4,500 in 'base' form. Although this excluded
weapons, radio and high-capacity heating/
cooling equipment, it was, nevertheless, a very
economical price for an armoured patrol vehicle.
Within a decade, more than 1,000 had been
produced, with approximately 1,500 vehicles
built by the time production came to an end in
the mid-1990s.

Initially, the Northern Ireland vehicles were
restricted to border patrols but, following the
escalation of violence in 1969, Shorlands were
used to patrol troubled areas of Belfast. All were
withdrawn in late 1969 and subsequently re-
issued to the Ulster Defence Regiment (UDR) in
1971, with a total of approximately 40 vehicles
being used; the first examples being operated by
the 6th Battalion (UDR).

The Mk 1 was superseded by the Mk 2, which
had an increased thickness of armour (up to
.33in [8.25mm]), and this, in turn, was replaced
in 1971 by the Mk 3, now powered by the six-
cylinder 2,625cc engine; an armoured-personnel
carrier (APC) variant was also offered using the
same chassis and front end, designated the SB-
301. The last of the original line, the Mk 4 and the
corresponding SB-401 Armoured Personnel
Carrier (APC), appeared in 1980 using the Series
III chassis and employing the 3.5-litre V8 engine
with Salisbury axles fitted with vacuum-
operated hydraulic differential locks.

Around 1986, the Series 5 was introduced,
based on the 110in (2.79m) coil-sprung

Defender chassis. By this time, Shorts were offering a choice of the original armoured patrol car (now identified as S.51), turreted (S.52), un-turreted personnel carriers (S.55) and an air-defence vehicle (S.53), which mounted two Blowpipe or Javelin surface-to-air missiles. The Series 5 featured power steering, a wider track, improved suspension, a tighter turning circle and improved performance with a top speed of 75mph (121kph). Although the engine compartment and radiator were obviously armoured, Shorts could also supply vehicles with what was described as a 'low-profile Land Rover-type armoured front' for operation in 'sensitive areas'. Optional extras included run-flat tyres, a machine-gun hatch in the S.55, armoured glass and a public-address system.

By the time production of the final variant, the Series 5, came to an end, the Shorland was in service with more than 38 countries, including Argentina, Botswana, Brunei, Burundi, Guyana, Kenya, Libya, Malaysia, Portugal, Seychelles, Thailand, United Arab

Emirates... and, of course, in Northern Ireland. Interest was also said to have come from the German Border Police and the Danish Army.

Glover Webb armoured patrol vehicle

Dating from around 1983, the Glover Webb armoured patrol vehicle (APV) was based on the One Ten chassis. It was said to be 'a highly-mobile, non-aggressive armoured personnel carrier with good anti-ballistic properties and a low profile'. Typical users included military and para-military forces, typically employed on internal security or riot-control duties, airfield perimeter control and escort duties. The conversion was fully approved by Land Rover and parts' commonality was claimed to be over 90%.

The welded hull was constructed from armoured sheet steel, and the windscreen and side windows were of 1.4in (35mm) multi-layer laminate glass, with a polycarbonate anti-spall liner. Glass-fibre composites were used to provide grenade and blast protection to the floor,

Above: The Shorland Series 5 was based on the 110in coil-sprung Defender chassis. The original armoured patrol car was joined by turreted and un-turreted personnel carriers, and an air-defence vehicle carrying a pair of Blowpipe Javelin surface-to-air missiles. *(TM)*

Above: The Glover Webb Hornet was constructed on the chassis of the One Ten and powered by Rover's V8 petrol engine. *(BM)*

and there was an additional belly plate under the cab area. The fuel tank was protected by the belly plate and was filled with explosion-protection foil.

Two doors provided access to the rear, where there was space for eight men. Gun ports and additional vision blocks could be fitted as required.

Optional equipment included a fire-extinguishing system, air conditioning, radio equipment, internal communication system, riot screens/folding visors, smoke or CS gas dischargers, and a power winch. The roof could be fitted with a machine-gun hatch suitable for mounting a general-purpose machine gun (GPMG).

The company also subsequently produced the Hornet, a lighter armoured vehicle on the Defender 110 chassis, which was suitable for commando and reconnaissance operations.

Hotspur Dragoon

Appearing for the first time at the 1984 British Army Equipment Exhibition, the Hotspur Dragoon 6484 APC was produced as a private venture by Hotspur Armoured Products Limited of Neath, South Wales. It was based on a modified and strengthened Defender 110 chassis with an additional powered axle, allowing a 6x6 or 6x4 drive-line.

The angular armoured steel hull enclosed the engine compartment and provided accommodation for 12 troops in the rear and a crew of two in the cab, with access via side or rear doors. The floor was armoured to protect against mine and grenade attacks. The hull was proof against 7.62mm rounds fired at 90º from 27yd (25m), and against point-blank attack from 9mm and .44in Magnum rounds. The multi-layer laminate glass windscreen and side windows included an anti-spaul polycarbonate layer; armoured shutters could be lifted over the windows for maximum protection. A light turret or machine gun hatch could be fitted over the rear compartment.

Optional equipment included a 24V electrical system, intercom, public address, smoke grenade launchers, power-assisted steering, run-flat tyres, and long-range, self-sealing fuel tanks.

Left: Shorland armoured car mounting a pair of Vigilant anti-aircraft missiles on the turret sides. *(TM)*

Left: Shorland Series 5 equipped with Blowpipe/Javelin anti-aircraft missiles. *(TM)*

Above and right:
The Shorland
Mk 4, and the
corresponding
SB-401 APC,
appeared in 1980,
using the Series III
chassis and the
3.5-litre V8 engine.
(ST)

Above: Shorland Mk 3 (SB-301) armoured personnel carrier, powered by the six-cylinder 2,625cc engine. *(TM)*

At the time of launch, the company was said to be considering the production of ambulance and communications variants.

Hotspur Sandringham

The Hotspur Sandringham APC was developed as a private venture by Hotspur Armoured Products Limited. It was derived from the Sandringham 6, a civilian 6x6 conversion of the Stage One, and offered excellent load-carrying and off-road performance. This was achieved through a combination of a V8 engine, permanent six-wheel drive and lockable centre differential. The conversion was fully approved by Land Rover and there was claimed to be over 90% commonality of parts.

A prototype was displayed at the 1980 British Army Equipment Exhibition and, by early 1981, the prototype had successfully completed a trials programme. Production started in 1982.

The basic APC was able to accommodate a crew of two in the cab together with eight fully-equipped troops in the rear compartment, seated on longitudinal benches along either side. The hull was of all-welded construction using Hotspur super-hard opaque steel armour, and was designed to provide protection from shell splinters and high-velocity rifle fire (typically, NATO 7.62mm ball round) at a minimum 44yds (40m) distance; the floor was protected against mine fragments and grenades. Access to the cab was provided by hinged doors fitted with large vision windows of composite glass and plastic construction, with separate polycarbonate anti-spall screens. Hinged armoured screens could also be specified for the windscreen and side windows. Access to the rear compartment was provided by two hinged doors fitted with fold-down steps. There were six firing ports fitted with vision blocks, two on each side of the vehicle and one in each rear door.

Armour was also fitted to the engine compartment and radiator. The wheels were equipped with run-flat bands which allowed limited operation on a punctured tyre.

Above: Long-wheelbase Defender APV1 with Makrolon composite armour for use in Northern Ireland. These vehicles were more heavily armoured than the standard machines equipped with the so-called vehicle protection kit (VPK). *(BM)*

The vehicle was offered with choice of wheelbase lengths at 125in (3.2m) and 139in (3.53m), identified as the S6 and S6E variants respectively.

Standard equipment included a fan ventilation system, interior lights, and a long-range 18 gallon (80 litre) explosion-proof fuel tank with a locking cap. Customers could also opt for an engine fire-extinguishing system, internal communication system, barricade ram, smoke or CS gas dischargers, power winch, heavy-duty alternator, diesel engine and a 6x4 drive-line.

Other body variants included a command and communications vehicle, field ambulance, long-distance patrol vehicle and fuel or water tanker. A commander's cupola could be installed in the roof at the rear, designed to mount a general-purpose machine gun (GPMG). It was also possible to adapt the basic Hotspur as a gun tractor or gun/missile platform.

Penman Engineering Skirmisher and Hussar

Designed by Penman Engineering, the Skirmisher 4x4 and Hussar 6x6 armoured vehicles were intended for military and security roles, including ambulance, command vehicle, escort or prisoner transport, and patrol reconnaissance duties. The basis of the vehicle was the V8-powered, coil-sprung One Ten and Defender 110, with the 6x6 drive-line conversion for the Hussar.

Offering slightly better ballistic protection than so-called non-aggressive armoured bodies such as the Glover Webb and Hotspur, the angular welded armoured-steel body of the Hussar was proof against high-velocity 7.62mm rounds and machine gun fire at 90° from 27yd (25m). The vehicle was designed to accommodate 12 men in the

rear, together with a two-man crew; a roof-mounted turret or machine-gun hatch could be fitted. The smaller Skirmish could carry eight men in the rear compartment plus a two-man crew in the cab.

Both vehicles offered similar levels of protection. The windows and windscreen were of multi-layer laminate glass with polycarbonate anti-spall screens, and there were armoured shutters. Vision blocks were fitted along each side as well as in the rear access doors and all of the doors were constructed to the same ballistic standard as the hull. Floor armour provided protection from mine fragments and grenades. The engine compartment was also protected.

Optional equipment included self-sealing fuel tanks, public-address system, night vision facilities, multiple grenade launchers, 24V electrical system, and split-rim wheels with run-flat tyres.

Other armoured Land Rovers

A small number of armoured para-military Land Rovers have been produced by Alvis and supplied to UK law-enforcement agencies, including the Metropolitan Police.

Similar vehicles, known as Tangi and produced in a range of types, have been built on a reinforced version of the Defender 110 chassis, powered either by the V8 petrol engine or the Td5 diesel, for use in Northern Ireland. Rear bodies were constructed from armoured steel with appliqué armoured panels. Makrolon composite-armour panels were used to protect the engine compartment and radiator. Tangi was preceded by a locally-produced conversion known as Simba which consisted of a Series III chassis carrying a welded-steel armoured hull at the rear. The vehicle was mounted on the heavy-duty springs

Above: At times, the security situation in Northern Ireland also demanded that the civil police be equipped with armoured vehicles and the current such vehicle is the Tangi. *(BM)*

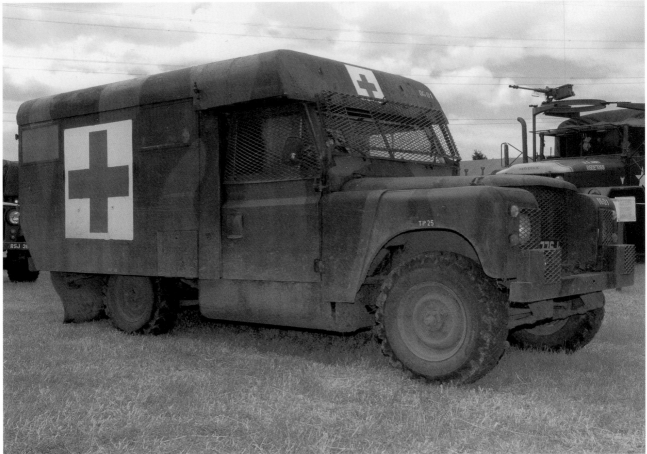

and larger wheels of the civilian forward-control models.

In 2003, an armoured 6x6 was produced by Jaguar Land Rover (Poland) and was demonstrated to the Polish Armed Forces in 2004. Based on the Australian-designed Perentie Defender 130 chassis and known as the Perentie Huzar, the vehicle is powered by the 2.5-litre turbo-diesel engine driving all six wheels through a five-speed gearbox. Fitted with modular armour, including top protection, it is eventually to be offered in three variants: the A-model, based on the Defender 130, the B-model which is derived from the Defender 110 and the smaller C-model which uses the Defender 90 chassis.

The Turkish Otokar firm also offers armoured Land Rovers for military, para-military and internal security roles. The 'discreetly armoured station wagon' looks almost like a standard Defender 110, whilst the more military-looking Akrep lightweight attack/defence vehicle and APC derivatives incorporate Defender automotive components in a heavy-duty armoured body. Standard variants of the APC, which is similar in appearance to the Shorland Mk 5, include ambulance and workshop vehicles. See page 186.

Appliqué armour

Land Rover 'lightweights' and Series III vehicles used in Northern Ireland were frequently fitted with the vehicle protection kit (VPK). This consisted of a hardtop, appliqué composite GRP and Makrolon ballistic-protection panels for the doors, sills and bonnet. Also an armoured shield for the windscreen with wire-mesh screens over the windows and lights. Two doors were fitted at the rear and a two-man hatch was installed in the roof.

British troops in Iraq are equipped with more than 300 of the so-called 'snatch' vehicles, a Land Rover Defender XD with composite glass-fibre armour. Although the armour is supposed to be resistant to penetration by rifle fire, it has been noted that the insurgents have weapons which 'go right through the composite'.

A new demountable armour system (DAS) is available for the Defender which has been designed by Labbe. The DAS, intended for use by aid agencies and others working in war zones, consists of a kit of armoured components which can be attached to a base vehicle as required. For the armour to be fitted, the vehicle requires a special heavy-duty bulkhead.

Above: The 6x6 Land Rover Hussar was produced by Penman Engineering. The hull provided accommodation for 14 men and mounted a rotating turret. *(BM)*

Top left: The Polish Huzar is based on the Perentie 6x6 conversion of the Defender 130 and first appeared in 2003. There will eventually be three variants available. *(BM)*

Bottom left: The Makrolon composite armour vehicle protection kit (VPK) was widely used in Northern Ireland to provide some protection to crews from small arms fire. *(ST)*

4.1 | Minerva

The Belgian Minerva car company was established in 1899 by Sylvain de Jong, a Dutchman living in Antwerp. De Jong started manufacturing bicycles in 1897 using the name Minerva, the Roman goddess of wisdom, war and crafts. In 1899, he graduated to motorcycles, exhibiting a prototype 'voiturette' and a light van at the Antwerp Cycle Show. The company's first car, a 6hp four-cylinder machine in the Panhard style, appeared in 1902.

  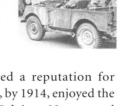  

Previous spread:
A superbly restored Minerva being displayed by its enthusiastic owner at a Beltring, Kent military vehicle show. *(ST)*

Minerva vehicles acquired a reputation for quality and reliability and, by 1914, enjoyed the patronage of the Kings of Belgium, Norway and Sweden. At the outbreak of World War One the Minerva factory began building improvised armoured cars for the Belgian Army. That was until Antwerp was over-run by the Germans on 9 October 1914.

In 1922 the company acquired a factory in Mortsel, a suburb of Antwerp, and in 1924 it started producing commercial vehicles following the acquisition of Auto Traction. After the death of De Jong in 1927 the company went into decline and, in 1934, was forced to restructure. A year later the new company was taken over by Mathieu Van Roggen's Impéria company. Commercial vehicles continued to be produced up to the outbreak of World War Two but from June 1940, the Mortsel factory was used by the German Erla-Maschinenwerk Gmbh organisation for the repair of military aircraft.

When peace returned Minerva quickly went back to commercial vehicle production, but lacked the resources to design and produce a new motorcar and the Mortsel facility was under-utilised.

In common with the other armies of newly-liberated Europe, Belgium received quantities of war surplus MB/GPW Jeeps, supplementing these with militarised post-war Willys CJ-2A and Universal CJ-3A Jeeps. By the end of the decade the Jeeps were starting to wear out, and the Belgian Army started seeking a replacement. Van Roggen was keen to secure the contract but the company was not in a position to design and build a vehicle from scratch. In early 1951 he secured a licence to build Land Rovers in Belgium and the Rover/Minerva consortium won a contract to supply the Belgian Army with an initial quantity of 2,500 vehicles. Over a period of four years this was increased to 10,000.

Rover agreed to provide technical assistance and to supply CKD (completely knocked-

down) kits to Minerva, including the engine, chassis, axles, transmission and the bulkhead pressing. The complete body was sourced locally, as were the lighting equipment, hood, tyres, body fittings, fuel tanks and upholstery. Contemporary Minerva literature stated that 63% of the content was of Belgian origin.

The Minerva TT was initially based on the 80in (2.03m) Series I cargo vehicle; after 1954, coinciding with the model change in the UK, the wheelbase was increased to 86in (2.18m). Early models used the standard Land Rover chassis, but later production was said to feature a boxed-in frame manufactured in Belgium and this lacked the power take-off hole in the rear cross-member.

Under the bonnet was the standard 1,997cc Rover F-head 58bhp four-cylinder engine, coupled to a four-speed gearbox and two-speed transfer case. The steering mechanism was by Burman and again, aside from being positioned on the left, was unchanged from the UK product.

Above: Although a standard Series I in most respects, the side view shows the curious angled front wings which were a distinctive feature of the Minerva. *(PW)*

Left: Minervas often carried a jerrycan on the rear in the style of the World War Two Jeep. *(PW)*

Axles, too, were the standard Solihull product, mounting one-piece 16in wheels shod with 6.00x16 cross-country tyres.

The major difference was in the locally-produced body which, although it was still recognisably a Land Rover - differed considerably from the UK model, most notably by being constructed from steel, which brought a weight penalty of more than 150lb (68kg).

In appearance the most obvious change was the rather ungainly slope-fronted wings, which were apparently easier to produce with simple tools than the rounded, pressed wings of the UK original. The radiator grille was narrower and, in place of the familiar 'T'-shaped mesh panel, there was a framed grille with the mesh running at 45° rather than 90°. There were separate pressed-steel slotted panels on either side under the headlamps. At the top of the grille a large cast badge was fitted showing the helmeted head of the goddess Minerva, with the legend 'Licence Rover' or the familiar Land Rover oval underneath. The distinctive external corner

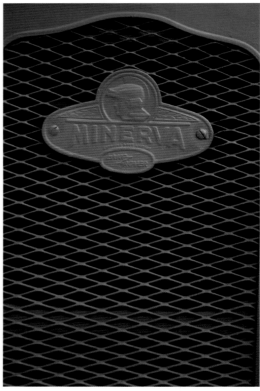

pieces and capping strips found on the doors and rear bodywork of the UK-built aluminium-bodied Land Rovers remained but, like the earliest UK 80in (2.03m) models, there were no vertical corner trims at the rear.

At the rear, the hinged tailgate was replaced by a fixed panel some two-thirds of the body height, carrying a jerrycan holder and sometimes a spare wheel. Most vehicles were also fitted with a military-type towing jaw. A pigtail-type towing eye was fitted to the front bumper above the chassis member.

Inside, there were two square-backed front seats with a toolbox between them. An additional inward-facing seat was fitted in the rear, on the right-hand wing box, with vertical grab handles attached to the rear panel. Weather equipment included a one-piece top and rear enclosure, with an attached roll-up rear panel glazed with two small transparent panes.

As in the UK, the electrical system was of the standard 12V pattern using two 6V, 120Ah batteries. Sidelights were mounted low-down on the front wings, and there was a single combined rear and brake light, together with a trailer socket fitted to the back panel. Flashing direction indicators were a standard fitting from 1952, being placed alongside the sidelights at the front, and on the bodywork corners at the rear.

From October 1953, with some design changes, the vehicle was also offered on the commercial market as an open cargo vehicle or short-wheelbase station wagon; unlike the military variants both were fitted with a standard tailgate.

The Minerva company went into liquidation in 1958, but it is a testament to Minerva that when replacement with VW Iltis vehicles started in 1985, a total of 2,492 original vehicles were still in service.

Variants

Alongside the standard cargo/utility vehicle, there were a 24V FFR (fitted for radio) variant with screened electrical system, and a two-

Above: Even as late as 1985 some 2,500 Minervas remained in service and many were sold from war reserve stock with very low mileage showing. *(PW)*

Right: In-service Minerva with the gunner manning a .30 calibre Browning machine gun. *(BM)*

Below: A full set of sidescreens and tilt could be fitted to provide weather protection. Note the civilian-type bumper fitted to this vehicle. *(PW)*

stretcher field ambulance similar to the British Series I with extending stretcher equipment and a hood extension at the rear. On these vehicles, the spare wheel was carried horizontally ahead of the radiator. A number of dual-control vehicles were built for use by military driving schools.

A small number of vehicles were converted for the parachute/commando role, armed with three 7.62mm FN MAG machine guns. Other modifications included strengthened suspension, outboard headlamps alongside an armoured shuttered grille, wing-mounted black-out lights, front-mounted spare wheel, armoured-glass aero-type screens, a rear stowage basket, and side-mounted grab handles. The vehicle was not fitted with doors.

Other armed vehicles, intended for the airfield defence role, carried .30 calibre or 7.62mm machine guns.

In 1980, a total of 13 vehicles were equipped to carry the MILAN anti-tank missile.

Production

Production started on 12 September 1951 with some 500 workers employed on the production line, from which 50 vehicles a day emerged. A total of 1,895 examples had been constructed by July 1952 when the chassis number prefix was changed to reflect the 1953 model year.

Many brand-new vehicles were immediately put into war reserve store by the Belgian Army and were gradually introduced into service until well into the 1980s. This led to the curious situation of Belgian Army units being issued with 'brand new' 25-year old Minervas, often serving alongside newer Series III vehicles… and also led to some examples with very low mileage being sold to collectors in virtually 'as new' condition.

A dispute between Minerva and Land Rover led to the cancellation of the production licence

Below: A small number of vehicles were converted for the parachute/ commando role, and armed with three FN MAG 7.62mm machine guns. The spare wheel was relocated to the front bumper in the style of the British 'Pink Panthers'. *(PW)*

Right and below:
Commando vehicles were usually armed with either three Browning .30in calibre or three FN MAG 7.62mm machine guns, the two at the front protected behind an armoured screen. *(PW)*

Above: This Belgian Army M113 engineer fitters' vehicle has lifted the Minerva to allow access to the chassis. *(BM)*

in 1954, although a further 270 kits were supplied in 1955 and 630 in 1956 under the terms of a settlement agreed between the two companies. Total military production was 5,921, with a total of 9905 vehicles constructed before production ceased on 30 October 1956; of these, 8,805 were of the 80in (2.03m) wheelbase and 1,100 were 86in (2.18m).

By 1956 Minerva had produced all-terrain vehicles to the company's designs; the TT-C20 (80in [2.03m]) and the TT-C22 (86in [2.18m])

models were intended for the civilian market and the TT-M20 for the military. Despite a somewhat familiar appearance there was no Land Rover input. The vehicles were powered by a US-built Continental engine of 2,295cc producing 59bhp. Despite innovative unitary construction - engine, transmission and front axle mounted on a removable subframe - neither was particularly successful and the Belgian Army continued to buy Land Rovers direct from the UK.

Technical specification
Minerva TT; 1952 to 56
Typical nomenclature: truck, 1/4 ton, cargo, 4x4; Minerva 'licence Rover' TT.

Engine: Rover; four cylinders; 1,997cc; overhead inlet valves, side exhaust; petrol; power output, 52bhp at 4,000rpm; torque, 101 lbf/ft at 1,500rpm.
Transmission: 4F1Rx2; part-time 4x4.
Steering: recirculating ball, worm and nut.
Suspension: live axles on multi-leaf semi-elliptical springs; hydraulic double-acting telescopic shock absorbers.
Brakes: hydraulic; drums all-round.
Construction: steel ladder chassis with pressed/fabricated-steel body.
Electrical system: 12V or 24V.

Dimensions
Length, 141in (3.6m) (including jerrycan holder and rear-mounted spare wheel), 129in (3.3m) (without jerrycan and spare wheel).
Width, 61in (1.56m);
Height, 74in (1.9m) (top up), 55in (1.4m) (top and windscreen folded).
Wheelbase, 80in; 86in (2.03m; 2.18m).
Ground clearance, 8.5in (22cm).
Weight, (unladen) 2,706lb (1,227kg), (laden) 4,004lb (1,816kg).

Performance
Average speed, (road) 55mph (88.5kph); (cross country) 15mph (24kph).
Range of action, 195 miles (314km).
Approach angle, 50°;
Departure angle, 50°.
Fording depth, 21in (53cm).

4.2 | Otokar

Established in 1963, the Otokar company started out producing Magirus-Deutz buses under licence and has grown to become one of the major automotive manufacturers in Turkey. During the 1970s the company was purchased by the Koc Group and, in the mid-1980s, started to produce armoured security vehicles. By 1987 Otokar had negotiated an agreement to produce Land Rover Defenders in Turkey, initially for the Turkish armed forces.

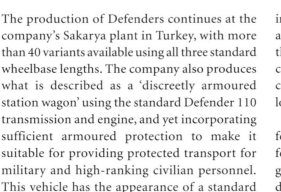

The production of Defenders continues at the company's Sakarya plant in Turkey, with more than 40 variants available using all three standard wheelbase lengths. The company also produces what is described as a 'discreetly armoured station wagon' using the standard Defender 110 transmission and engine, and yet incorporating sufficient armoured protection to make it suitable for providing protected transport for military and high-ranking civilian personnel. This vehicle has the appearance of a standard Defender 110.

Alongside these products, Otokar has developed a range of 4x4 tactical light armoured wheeled vehicles, using some technologies licensed from Land Rover as well as from the US company AM General.

Armoured patrol vehicle

The Otokar armoured patrol vehicle is a light 4x4, similar in style to the Shorland SS5,

intended for military and security roles. Badged as a 'Land Rover', the manufacturers claim that the vehicle shares around 80% of mechanical components with the Defender 110, which, of course, brings considerable practical and logistical advantages.

Power is provided by the Land Rover 300 Tdi four-cylinder turbo-diesel engine, driving all four wheels through a five-speed manual gearbox and Land Rover power train. The heavy-duty live axles are suspended on long-travel, dual-rate coil springs. Axle location is by radius arms and Panhard rod at the front with tubular trailing links at the rear, in combination with a centrally-mounted 'A' frame. Run-flat tyres are a standard fitment.

The welded steel hull provides protection from 7.62mm NATO ball ammunition fired at point-blank range, and machine-pressed glass-fibre composite armour plates under the floor area help to deflect blast from anti-personnel mines, grenades and improvised explosive

Above: Otokar Defender 90 equipped with the venerable M40 106mm recoiless rifle. *(PW)*

Left: Otokar armoured patrol vehicle with a small armoured turret. *(PW)*

Top: Crew-cabbed Otokar Defender 130. *(PW)*

Above: Otokar 110 ambulance. *(PW)*

devices. The driver has a two-piece multi-layer laminate windscreen. Small windows are set into the door tops and all windows are protected to the same ballistic standards as the hull and include anti-spall polycarbonate liners. Access to the rear compartment is obtained by two side-hung doors, whilst armoured doors allow easy access to the interconnected cab. The hull also includes small side and rear vision/ firing ports.

Air-conditioning and internal ventilation are provided as standard equipment.

The standard APC can accommodate six fully-equipped personnel on inward-facing bench seats, together with a crew of two in the cab. The vehicle can be fitted with a roof hatch or a simple open turret, typically mounting a 7.62mm or .50 calibre machine gun. Other variants include ambulance, workshop, command, airfield security and internal security vehicles.

Optional equipment includes a barricade remover, public address system, searchlights and electrically-operated winch the vehicle remains in production at the time of writing.

Akrep attack/defence vehicle

Introduced in the early-1990s, and also still in production today, the Otokar Akrep is a light armoured reconnaissance vehicle with 70% commonality of mechanical components with the Defender 110, notably sharing the 300 Tdi turbo-charged diesel engine, four-speed transmission, axles and suspension.

Left: Otokar Defender 130 equipped as an anti-aircraft missile carrier. *(PW)*

Below: Otokar Defender 110 fitted with a battlefield radar system. *(PW)*

Ideal for escort, reconnaissance and border-control duties, the Akrep is available as an APC, mobile ground surveillance vehicle, and internal security vehicle and as a weapons platform with a choice of a single 7.62mm general-purpose machine gun (GPMG) in an overhead mount or a turret-mounted 12.7mm machine gun. The vehicle is also available with a remote-controlled roof turret mounting two 7.62mm GPMGs with a forward-looking infra-red vision system to allow observation and target acquisition.

The vehicle has an angular, low-silhouette armoured-steel box hull with internal polyurethane thermal and acoustic insulation; the front-mounted engine has full armoured protection. A single side-hung door provides access from the rear and there are forward doors for the driver and co-driver. The hull is constructed from certified, high-hardness steel and provides protection from 7.62mm NATO ball ammunition fired at 90° incidence at point-blank range. The driver is provided with a multi-layer laminate windscreen and side windows with anti-spall polycarbonate liners; small vision ports are provided in the rear body and in the rear door. Firing ports are also fitted.

Standard equipment includes air-conditioning, heater/demister, run-flat tyres, infra-red and black-out driving lamps. An electric winch, smoke grenade dischargers communications equipment and satnav system are also available at extra cost.

Right: The Otokar
Akrep is available in
a number of variants.
(PW)

Below: The interior
of the Otokar
armoured patrol
vehicle. *(PW)*

Technical specifications
Otokar armoured patrol vehicle; 1992 to date
Typical nomenclature: truck, (1,000kg), armoured personnel carrier, 4x4; Land Rover-Otokar APV.

Engine: Land Rover 300 Tdi; four cylinders; 2,506cc; overhead valves; direct-injection turbo-charged diesel; power output, 111bhp at 4,000rpm; torque, 195 lbf/ft at 1,800rpm.
Transmission: 5F1Rx2; full-time 4x4; centre lockable differential.
Steering: recirculating ball, worm and nut; servo power assisted.
Suspension: reinforced live axles on long-travel, dual-rate coil springs; axle location by Panhard rod at the front, and 'A' frame at the rear; hydraulic double-acting telescopic shock absorbers.
Brakes: dual-circuit servo-assisted hydraulic; discs all round.
Construction: monocoque welded body of armoured-steel.
Electrical system: 12V, 24V.

Dimensions
Length, 163in (4.14m).
Width, 71in (1.8m).
Height, (without turret) 89in (2.3m), (with turret) 108in (2.7m).
Wheelbase, 110in (2.8m).
Ground clearance, 8in (20cm).
Weight, 6,600lb (2,944kg) (unladen), 7,920lb (3,592.5kg) (laden).

Performance
Maximum speed, (road) 77mph (124kph); (cross country) 30mph (48kph).
Range of action, 275 miles (422.6km).
Approach angle, 48⁰.
Departure angle, 32⁰.
Fording depth, 24in (61cm).

Otokar Akrep attack/defence vehicle; 1992 to date
Typical nomenclature: armoured reconnaissance vehicle, 4x4; Land Rover-Otokar Akrep.

Engine: Land Rover 300 Tdi; four cylinders; 2,506cc; overhead valves; direct-injection turbo-charged diesel; power output, 111bhp at 4,000rpm; torque, 195 lbf/ft at 1,800rpm.
Transmission: 5F1Rx2; full-time 4x4; centre lockable differential.
Steering: recirculating ball, worm and nut; servo power assisted.
Suspension: reinforced live axles on long-travel, dual-rate coil springs; axle location by Panhard rod at the front, and 'A' frame at the rear; hydraulic double-acting telescopic shock absorbers.
Brakes: dual-circuit servo-assisted hydraulic; discs all round.
Construction: monocoque welded body of armoured steel.
Electrical system: 12V, 24V.

Dimensions
Length, 165in (4.2m).
Width, (without side-mounted spare wheel) 75in (1.9m), (with spare wheel fitted) 82in (2.1m).
Height, (without turret) 79in(2m), (with turret) 98in(2.5m).
Wheelbase, 106in (2.7m).
Ground clearance, 9in (23cm).
Weight, 7,040lb (3,193kg) (unladen), 7,920lb (3,592.5kg) (laden).

Performance
Maximum speed, (road) 77mph (124kph); (cross country) 30mph (48kph).
Range of action, 365 miles (587km).
Approach angle, 67⁰.
Departure angle, 54⁰.
Fording depth, 24in (61cm).

Below: Crew-cabbed Otokar Defender 130, showing the shelter body (left) and the extended open cargo body (right). *(PW)*

4.3 | Perentie

The Australian Army had been using locally-assembled Series IIA Land Rovers since the early 1960s when the type had been introduced. Produced by Leyland Australia, and later Jaguar-Rover Australia (JRA), they were largely similar to the UK-built vehicles, differing mainly by having a full-width brushguard at the front, over-sized angular front wing cut-outs and protected tail lights.

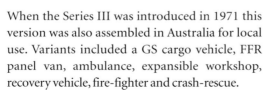

When the Series III was introduced in 1971 this version was also assembled in Australia for local use. Variants included a GS cargo vehicle, FFR panel van, ambulance, expansible workshop, recovery vehicle, fire-fighter and crash-rescue.

During 1981 JRA started development work on a heavy-duty 6x6 truck based on components of the Land Rover 110 and capable of accommodating a payload up to 6,614lb (3,000kg). Prototypes were based on a development vehicle produced by SMC Engineering Limited of Bristol in south-west England.

At around the same time the Australian Army announced initial studies for what was known as 'Project Perentie', a scheme to procure 25,000 1-tonne and 400 2-tonne vehicles in a range of standard variants during the period 1987 to 1990. Seven companies submitted tenders, and three of these were selected to provide test vehicles for extended trials, including JRA and the Jeep Corporation.

The standard 110, known as the MC2 4x4 Perentie, was offered in the 1-tonne 4x4 class, but for the 2-tonne vehicle JRA proposed an upgraded version of the 110 heavy-duty 6x6 which was already in production at the company's Moorebank plant, near Sydney. At the conclusion of the trials JRA received contracts for both types of vehicle.

1-ton MC2

The 110 was locally-constructed, and was modified in a number of small ways. The chassis was lengthened at the rear to allow the spare wheel to be carried under the body, two jerrycans were mounted on the rear cross-member and the chassis was galvanised. The major changes were under the bonnet, where power was provided by a 3,900cc Isuzu 4BD1 four-cylinder diesel engine, driving through the four-speed transmission of an early model Range Rover.

192

Above and left:
Intended for use by Australian special forces, the Perentie 6x6 MC2 long-range patrol vehicle, was fitted with a non-demountable body.
(BM)

Standard variants included soft-top cargo vehicle, hardtop and soft-top FFR commun-ications vehicles, personnel carrier/station wagon, command vehicle and soft-top surveillance vehicle - the latter being uprated for a 2,645lb (1,200kg) payload. A proportion of vehicles was fitted with a front-mounted Thomas electric-powered winch for vehicle self-recovery.

Production started in 1987, with the first vehicles delivered during August of that year.

2-ton MC2

Although it was also based on the 110, with which it shared considerable component commonality, the MC2 6x6 Perentie was unique to Australia. The vehicle was wider and longer than anything which Land Rover had produced in the UK. It was similarly powered by the Isuzu 4BD1 diesel engine, driving through a Range Rover transmission, although the 4BD1 engine was now

Left: This MC2 special patrol vehicle, photographed in Afghanistan, is equipped with MILAN anti-tank missiles, a .50 calibre Browning heavy machine gun in the rear, and a 7.62mm general-purpose machine gun on a scuttle mount. *(PW)*

turbo-charged which produced an almost 50% increase in power output.

The chassis was also galvanised but was designed especially for the six-wheel drive vehicle, employing deeper side-members and cross-members at the front. A fabricated rear section of rectangular-shaped steel tubing was designed to support the rear bogie.

The front axle was suspended on the standard long-travel coil springs, whilst the rear bogie employed a pair of Salisbury 8HA axles mounted on multi-leaf semi-elliptical springs fitted with a rubber-bushed load-sharing rocker. The rocker was cranked to allow the long springs to overlap, bringing the axles as close together as possible.

Drive to the rear-most axle was by means of a separate propeller shaft from the transfer case power take-off, using the technique which had been devised to drive the powered trailer for

Above and right:
Alongside the special
patrol vehicle,
standard variants
for the 6x6 MC2
Perentie include
a steel-cabbed
pick-up truck;
12-seat personnel
carrier; water tanker;
FFR air-defence
vehicle; gun tractor;
four-stretcher
ambulance;
box body; and
shelter carrier.
(TM [top] BM [right])

the forward-control 101. The propeller shaft passed over the second axle and was articulated by means of a constant-velocity joint, allowing extreme articulation of the two rear axles. Normal drive was 4x4 using the front and centre axles. Drive to the rear-most axle was actioned by means of a vacuum-operated dog clutch. Where the prototype and some early commercial examples had used the standard 110 front axle, the production military vehicles

Technical specifications
MC2 4x4 Perentie; 1987
Typical nomenclature: truck, 1,000kg, cargo, 4x4; Land Rover MC2.

Engine: Isuzu 4BD1; four cylinders; 3,856cc; direct-injection diesel; overhead valves; power output, 84bhp at 3,200rpm; torque, 180 lbf/ft at 1,900rpm.
Transmission: 4F1Rx2; full-time 4x4; centre lockable differential.
Steering: recirculating ball, worm and nut.
Suspension: reinforced live axles on long-travel, dual-rate coil springs; axle location by Panhard rod at the front, and 'A' frame at the rear; hydraulic double-acting telescopic shock absorbers.
Brakes: dual-circuit servo-assisted hydraulic; front discs brakes, drums at rear.
Construction: reinforced welded box-section galvanised-steel chassis; steel-framed aluminium-panelled body.
Electrical system: 12V.

Dimensions
Length, 192in (4.9m).
Width, 70in (1.8m).
Height, (top of cab), 81in (2.01m).
Wheelbase, 110in (2.8m).
Ground clearance, 8in (20cm).
Weight, 4,950lb (2,245kg) (unladen), 7,040lb (3,193kg) (laden).

Performance
Maximum speed, (road) 72mph (116kph); (cross country) 30mph (48kph).
Range of action, 280 miles (450km).
Approach angle, 30⁰.
Departure angle, 26⁰.
Fording depth, 24in (61cm).

MC2 6x6 Perentie; 1989 to 98
Typical nomenclature: truck, 2,000kg, cargo, 6x6; Land Rover MC2 heavy-duty.

Engine: Isuzu 4BD1-T; four cylinders; 3,856cc; direct-injection turbo-charged diesel; overhead valves; power output, 115bhp at 3,200rpm; torque, 231 lbf/ft at 1,900rpm.
Transmission: 4F1Rx2; full-time 4x4, selectable 6x6; centre lockable differential.
Steering: variable-ratio worm and peg; power assisted.
Suspension: reinforced live axles; long-travel, dual-rate coil springs at front, with axle location by Panhard rod; twin longitudinal dual-rate semi-elliptical multi-leaf springs linked via shackles to cranked rocker beam at rear.
Brakes: dual-circuit servo-assisted hydraulic; front discs brakes, drums at rear.
Construction: reinforced welded box-section galvanised-steel chassis; steel-framed aluminium-panelled body.
Electrical system: 12V, 24V.

Dimensions
Length, 242in (6.15m).
Width, 81in (2.05m) (maximum).
Height, (top of cab), 82in (2.1m).
Wheelbase, 120in (3.0m); bogie centres, 35in (89cm).
Ground clearance, 7.75in (19.7cm).
Weight, 8,052lb (3,652kg) (unladen), 12,452lb (5,648kg) (laden).

Performance
Maximum speed, (road) 60mph (96.6kph); (cross country) 25mph (40kph).
Range of action, 400 miles (644km).
Approach angle, 37⁰;
Departure angle, 25⁰.
Fording depth, 24in (61cm).

used axles with a wider track. The axles were fitted with lower ratio differential gears to accommodate the increased weight of the vehicle. Most vehicles were fitted with a front-mounted Thomas T9000M 8,818lb (4,000kg) electric-powered self-recovery winch and, like the 4x4, the spare wheel was mounted under the chassis at the rear.

Early civilian 6x6 chassis had been fitted with the standard 110 cab, but production military vehicles were mounted with a larger cab which was increased in length, width and headroom. A one-piece windscreen was fitted.

Standard variants included a steel-cabbed pick-up truck; 12-seat personnel carrier; water tanker; FFR air-defence vehicle, mounting Rapier or RBS-70 anti-aircraft missiles; gun tractor; four-stretcher ambulance and box body.

There was also a shelter carrier, for workshop, electronic repair and maintenance roles. Much of this versatility was obtained by virtue of the modular design which allowed different bodies to be fitted to a common chassis.

There was also a long-range patrol vehicle, often seen carrying a motorcycle hung on the rear. The vehicle had a non-demountable body and was intended for use by Australian special forces.

Deliveries of the 6x6 Perentie to the Australian Army started in March 1989 although the vehicle had been available to domestic commercial buyers for some time. It was also offered for defence sales worldwide, described as the 'Land Rover 110 heavy duty', with the standard Buick-derived Rover 3.5-litre V8 petrol engine as an option in place of the Isuzu diesel.

4.4 | Santana

The Linares-based Santana Company was established by the Spanish Government as Metalurgica de Santa Ana SA in February 1955, initially to construct agricultural machinery to bring much-needed employment to the depressed Jaén region in the province of Andalusia. In 1956 the company reached agreement with Land Rover to produce vehicles under licence, with Rover in the UK owning 49% of the shares in Santana.

Although the production volume was initially modest the company has grown to become a significant supplier to the Spanish-speaking market, with exports to South America and North Africa commencing in 1962. By 1980, Santana was producing 18,000 vehicles a year.

At the time that the licence was granted to MSA - Santana was actually the company's trademark - the Series I was still in production at Solihull. For various logistical reasons there was no Series I production in Spain. The first Spanish-built Land Rovers were Series IIs produced from CKD (completely-knocked-down) kits with some locally manufactured components, which went on sale in 1959. For the first 1,500 units constructed the local content was required to reach 75%, rising to 95% by the time 2,500 vehicles had been completed.

Although the complete UK model range was not available to Spanish buyers, the vehicles were very similar to the Solihull product. It was not until the Spanish Army started to buy Santana-built Land Rovers that the vehicles started to emerge almost as a brand in their own right, ultimately developing differently to the UK product. At first the Spanish Army simply purchased standard 88in (2.24m) and 109in (2.77m) Series II vehicles, but two special military models appeared in the early 1970s, developed to suit the requirements of the Spanish Army. The first was an 88in (2.24m) 1,102lb (500kg) 'lightweight', the other a similar 109in (2.77m) vehicle rated at 2,204lb (1,000kg).

At the same time Santana continued to produce civilian and commercial Land Rovers, including the forward-control 1300 - which was also bodied as a military ambulance – also Series II and III cargo and station wagon models. Santana never used the Rover V8 petrol engine which became such an important feature of the modern Solihull vehicles, but the company was the first to use a turbo-diesel, offering a 2,286cc four-cylinder unit in the 'Super T' models as

early as 1983. Santana also fitted the flush radiator grille that Solihull first used on the Stage One, as well as the one-piece windscreen which became a distinctive feature of the Ninety, One Ten and Defender models.

Over the years Land Rover reduced their shareholding in the company to 23%. In 1990 Land Rover disposed of all of the remaining shares and at the same time terminated the licence agreement. By that time Santana had produced 300,000 vehicles. The company continues to manufacture very similar vehicles, the current offering being the Defender-like PS10 which is available in both military and civilian versions.

Model 88

Known as the Model 88 Militar, the 1,102lb (500kg) 'lightweight' adopted a similar approach to that used for the British 'lightweight' with a body which could be quickly stripped for air-

portability. Development had started in 1969, with the first production example appearing in 1970. A total of 3,500 examples were constructed before production ceased in 1990.

With a curious-looking flattened front end, double bumpers, and cutaway angular wheel arches carrying tiny, recessed headlights, there was no mistaking the appearance of the Model 88. Power was provided by a Santana-built version of the 2,286cc four-cylinder petrol engine driving through a four-speed gearbox and two-speed transfer case, although a diesel engine option was also available. The front and rear axles used the same type of differential.

Both hardtop and soft-top versions were available and the Model 88 was adopted as the standard vehicle in its class by the Spanish Army. In standard form the Model 88 provided seating for two men in the front and either four men, on inward facing seats, or 1,102lb (500kg) of cargo in the rear. It was also suitable for towing a 2,203lb (1,000kg) trailer or light gun. Other

Above: Santana Model 109 Militar; note the characteristic cut-away wings and the lashing/ lifting eyes on the wheel hubs. *(BM)*

Above: Dating from 1970, the Santana Model 88 Militar was modelled on the British 'lightweight' and could be quickly stripped for air-portability. *(BM)*

variants included a hardtopped command or communications version, equipped with a 42Ah or 90Ah alternator, and weapons carrier versions mounting either the MILAN anti-tank missile, 106mm M40 recoilless rifle, 60mm mortar and 7.62mm or .50 calibre machine guns.

There was also a snorkel-equipped deep wading version designed for 74in (1.88m) immersion, using waterproofed ancillaries and a de-pressurised breather system for the engine, gearbox and axles. The vehicle's chassis was galvanised to resist corrosion.

In a reverse of the more usual approach to the development of civilian Land Rovers, in 1980 the Santana Model 88 was made available in civilian form as the 88 Ligero. It differed in a number of ways from the military version, most noticeably in the use of rectangular headlamps, the Series III grille and a fixed rollover bar.

Model 109

Similar in appearance to the Model 88 of which it was effectively a long-wheelbase variant, the 1-tonne Santana vehicle was identified as the Model 109 Militar, and was produced in both military and civilian versions. It was initially based on the Series IIA and then ultimately on the Series III. Buyers had a choice of the same 2,286cc four-cylinder petrol or diesel engines as were used in the Model 88, or a locally-produced 3,429cc six-cylinder petrol or diesel unit. All versions shared the same four-speed gearbox and

two-speed transfer case. Two fuel tanks gave a capacity of 25 gallons (127 litre), which resulted in a greatly increased range of operation.

It shared the curious flattened frontal appearance of the smaller Model 88 with its recessed headlamps and cutaway wheel arches. From the scuttle aft the vehicles were pure Land Rover.

The standard military variant was the basic eight to 10-seat troop or cargo carrier, available with either a hardtop or soft-top; it was also used as a weapons mount. There was also a communications vehicle available equipped with a hardtop, screened electrical equipment, oil cooler, and 50Ah or 90Ah alternators, fitted to suit a number of different radio configurations. A light recovery version had a folding 2,204lb (1,000kg) electrically-operated jib mounted in the cargo area. There was also an ambulance with a similar over-sized four-stretcher body to the standard British ambulances.

Like the Model 88, there was also a snorkel-equipped deep-wading version available and examples of this were used by the Spanish Marines.

The Model 109 entered production in 1973, and was supplied to the Armies of Spain, Egypt and Morocco. More than 2,000 vehicles were completed when production ceased with the end of Land Rover's involvement in 1990.

Santana S-2000

It is also worth mentioning that, in 1981, Santana also produced what could be considered a civilian version of the British 101 forward-control vehicle, designated S-2000.

Although the vehicle was rated at 4,409lb (2,000kg), it was powered by a six-cylinder petrol or diesel engine, rather than the V8 which was fitted into the military version. The wheelbase was identical to the British vehicle and the chassis was almost certainly based on that of Solihull's 101.

The S-2000 was fitted with a distinctive flat-panelled body, and available styles included a drop-side truck, personnel carrier or chassis-cab for special applications. In 1982 the Spanish Army used the open-cab type as a mount for the 20mm Oerlikon anti-aircraft cannon.

Technical specification
Santana Model 88 Militar; 1969 to 1990
Typical nomenclature: truck, 500kg, cargo, 4x4;
Land Rover/Santana Model 88.

Engine: Santana; four cylinders; 2,286cc; overhead valves; petrol; power output, 71bhp at 4,000rpm; torque, 120 lbf/ft at 2,500rpm. Optional 2,286cc diesel engine also available.
Transmission: 4F1Rx2; part-time 4x4.
Steering: recirculating ball, worm and nut.
Suspension: live axles on multi-leaf semi-elliptical springs; hydraulic double-acting telescopic shock absorbers.
Brakes: hydraulic; drums all-round.
Construction: steel ladder chassis with steel-framed aluminium body.
Electrical system: 24V.

Dimensions
Length, 146in (3.7m); width, 65in (1.7m);
Height, 81in (2.06m) (top up).
Wheelbase, 88in (2.24m).
Ground clearance, 8.25in (21cm).
Weight, (unladen) 2,974lb (1,349kg), (laden) 4,840lb (2,195kg).

Performance
Average speed, (road) 65mph (105kph);
(cross country) 30mph (48kph).
Range of action, 360 miles (579km).
Approach angle, 48⁰.
Departure angle, 32⁰.
Fording depth, 74in (1.88m) with special equipment.

Santana Model 109 Militar; 1973 to 1990
Typical nomenclature: truck, 1,000kg, cargo, 4x4;
Land Rover/Santana Model 109.

Engine: Santana; four cylinders; 2,286cc; overhead valves; petrol; power output, 71bhp at 4,000rpm; torque, 120 lbf/ft at 2,500rpm. Optional 2,286cc diesel and 3,429cc petrol or diesel engines also available.
Transmission: 4F1Rx2; part-time 4x4.
Steering: recirculating ball, worm and nut.
Suspension: live axles on multi-leaf semi-elliptical springs; hydraulic double-acting telescopic shock absorbers.
Brakes: hydraulic; drums all-round.
Construction: steel ladder chassis with steel-framed aluminium body.
Electrical system: 24V.

Dimensions
Length, 179in (4.55m); width, 65in (1.65m);
Height, 81in (2.1m) (top up).
Wheelbase, 109in (2.8m).
Ground clearance, 8.5in (22cm).
Weight, (unladen) 3,615lb (1,1640kg), (laden) 6,035lb (2,737.5kg).

Performance
Average speed, (road) 65mph (105kph);
(cross country) 30mph (48kph).
Range of action, 500 miles (805m).
Approach angle, 52⁰.
Departure angle, 31⁰.
Fording depth, 74in (1.88m) with special equipment.

Left: Santana Model 109 Militar with a factory-fitted hardtop and roofrack.
Note the extended double-height bumpers compared to those used on British vehicles.
(BM)

4.5 | Tempo

In 1926, two Hamburg-based locksmiths produced a motorcycle-based three-wheeled truck which they named Tempo. Among the customers for this machine were coal merchants Oscar Vidal and his father Max. Sufficiently taken by the potential of the Tempo, in 1928 the Vidals purchased the manufacturing rights and, with the engineer Otto Daus, established Vidal & Sohn to produce the three-wheeled Tempo Pony.

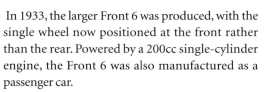

In 1933, the larger Front 6 was produced, with the single wheel now positioned at the front rather than the rear. Powered by a 200cc single-cylinder engine, the Front 6 was also manufactured as a passenger car.

A four-wheeled van was offered for sale in 1936, along with an equivalent car, but three-wheeled commercial vehicles were always in the majority and in 1937 Vidal were producing some 40% of all delivery vans sold in Germany.

In 1936 the all-wheel-drive G1200 military light car was introduced, remaining in production until 1939. Designed by Otto Daus, the vehicle featured independent suspension all round and was powered by two 2-cylinder engines of 596cc, one located at the rear and one at the front, each driving its respective axle through a four-speed gearbox. Marketed in 40 countries, the Tempo G1200 was sold to the Wehrmacht in small numbers and was also trialled by the British Army. Approximately 1,200 examples were produced.

During World War Two the Tempo E400 was the German Army's standardised three-wheeled load carrier.

After the war the A400 (later known as the Hanseat) three-wheeled light commercial vehicle went back into production, estate car versions of the vans remaining available until 1956. The four-wheeled Matador was introduced in 1949 and the three-wheeled Boy 880-1,100lb (400-500kg) truck was produced in 1950, and joined by the Wiking in 1953. In 1956, Oscar Vidal sold 50% of the company to Rheinstahl-Hanomag. Ten years later Rheinstahl-Hanomag acquired the remainder of Vidal, with the vehicles being marketed under the Hanomag name until 1970, then as Hanomag-Henschel until about 1974 when Hanomag became part of Mercedes-Benz.

The Land Rover story begins in early 1952, when the German Federal *Bundesgrenzschutz* (BGS) issued an invitation to tender for a six-seat cross-country vehicle intended to be used for

patrolling the border with East Germany. A number of domestic manufacturers were approached but showed little interest, all of them presumably being too busy with meeting civilian demand. In April 1952 the BGS conducted a series of trials which pitched seven examples of the home-grown Mercedes-Benz Unimog against seven 80in (2.03m) Series I export Land Rovers. Although the Land Rover was clearly the more suitable, it appears that the factory was not in a position to supply the required number of vehicles within a reasonable timescale and anyway the BGS was enthusiastic - or possibly even under an obligation - to purchase a German-produced vehicle. Vidal had already shown an interest in securing the contract, having already experimented with cross-country vehicles with the G1200 in the 1930s, but lacked the time and resources necessary to develop a new vehicle from scratch.

Aware of the licence-built Minerva vehicles being produced in Antwerp, Vidal approached Land Rover seeking a similar arrangement. At the end of 1952 Vidal & Sohn received a licence to assemble Land Rovers in Germany using body and other parts of local origin.

Between April and August 1953 somewhere between 100 and 189 vehicles were assembled in the Hamburg-Harburg factory using chassis,

Above: Post-1954 Tempo had a bonnet-mounted spare wheel. The high-sided body was of steel construction. *(JT)*

axles, gearboxes and power units supplied from Solihull. Although the bulkhead was supplied from the UK, as were the bonnet and grille, the remainder of the bodywork, which was generally of steel construction, was produced locally by Herbert Vidal & Company, owned by Oscar Vidal's brother.

Some sources suggest that there was a second order for 80in (2.03m) vehicles calling for a further 48 examples, but definitive information is not available.

In appearance the vehicle was unmistakably a Land Rover, but closer examination reveals considerable differences. Most noticeable is the high-sided rear body and the length of the doors, both of which reached to the bottom of the windscreen. A stowage box was provided across the bonnet for the removable side windows and a

Left and below: A
preserved post-
1954 Tempo. The
vehicle is UK based
but note that the
windows in the hood
are not to the
original pattern. *(JT)*

locker was built into the front/top of each front wing. The spare wheel was carried centrally on the rear, in the style of a Jeep. Rather than being removable, the canvas top was arranged to fold down. Door handles were sourced locally and differed from those used in the UK. There were flashing indicators on the sides of the front wings, with a flashing blue light and siren inboard of the wings and ahead of the radiator. An auxiliary switch panel was fitted on the dashboard above the standard Rover item. Some examples were fitted with a front-mounted capstan winch, and there were 'bumperettes' fitted to the cross-member at the rear, together with a radio antenna.

The wheels appear to have been the standard UK-produced one-piece steel rims, but the tyres were 6.00x16 rather than the 6.50x16 type used on the two-piece wheels of British Army Series Is.

Inside the body there were two tip-up seats for the driver and passenger (the centre seat was not fitted) with provision for four more men on inward-facing lateral benches in the rear. If a radio was carried, it was mounted between the front seats. A heater was fitted as standard equipment.

Power was provided by the standard 1,997cc four-cylinder petrol engine, driving through a Rover four-speed gearbox and two-speed transfer box. Although almost all of the under-bonnet components were of UK origin, a high-capacity Bosch generator was fitted. The electrical system featured a negative-earth return rather than the positive return of UK vehicles of the period.

In 1954, in line with changes made in the UK, the wheelbase was increased to 86in (2.18m) and a number of other changes were made, with the revised models designated '041'.

The spare wheel was moved to the bonnet and the stowage box for the side windows was removed; the windscreen hinges were set higher as on the revised UK vehicle. Although the wing-top lockers remained, stowage clips were also provided on the bonnet and wing tops for pioneer tools. Width indicators were fitted to the front wings. There were two fuel tanks, together with an auxiliary tank under the passenger seat, which doubled the original 11 gallons (50 litre) capacity. A jerrycan was carried at the rear alongside the spare wheel. The sidelights and indicators were combined in a single unit and mounted on the front faces of the wings. Changes were made to the instrument panel, with the auxiliary switches now placed to the left rather than above the standard instruments. Between 150 and 187 examples were produced in this form.

In 1956 the BGS allocated 100 of the best examples of Tempo Land Rovers to the newly-

Above: In original form, the Tempo was fitted with a storage box across the bonnet designed to accomodate the sidescreens. This was deleted in 1954. *(JT)*

Right: A radio-equipped Tempo of the *Bundeswehr*. Storage lockers were also incorporated in the front wings. *(JT)*

formed Bundeswehr, along with 10,000 former BGS personnel.

Vidal was keen to obtain further orders and actually produced two Series II-based vehicles as demonstrators. These were constructed on an 88in (2.24m) chassis; the body was of the slab-sided type. Additional width was inserted into the front wings to match the new, wider bulkhead design. Chassis number records also show that Vidal received two 109in (2.77m) Series I chassis in March 1958 although what became of these, is not known. Sadly, there were to be no further orders and production was terminated in 1956.

All future Bundeswehr Land Rovers were supplied directly from the UK and the Tempos were withdrawn from service during the mid-1960s.

Vidal had also hoped to be able to sell the vehicle in civilian guise, but contemporary catalogues suggest that they were simply marketing the standard 86in (2.18m) Rover product badged 'Tempo'. There is some uncertainty as to how many were actually purchased but, Vidal & Sohn continued to operate as the Land Rover distributor in Germany for many years.

Above: Interior of the Tempo showing the tipping seats at the front and lateral benches at the rear. *(JT)*

Technical specification
Tempo-Rover; 1953 to 1956
Typical nomenclature: field car, 1/4 ton, 6 seater, 4x4; Tempo-Rover.

Engine: Rover; four cylinders; 1,997cc; overhead inlet valves, side exhaust; petrol; power output, 52bhp at 4,000rpm; torque, 101 lbf/ft at 1,500rpm.
Transmission: 4F1Rx2; part-time 4x4.
Steering: recirculating ball, worm and nut.
Suspension: live axles on multi-leaf semi-elliptical springs; hydraulic double-acting telescopic shock absorbers.
Brakes: hydraulic; drums all-round.
Construction: steel ladder chassis with pressed/fabricated-steel body.
Electrical system: 12V.

Dimensions
Length, 147in (3.7m) (including rear-mounted spare wheel), 140in (3.6m) (without spare wheel).
Width, 61in (1.55m).
Height, 76in (1.93m) (top up), 56in (1.42m) (top and windscreen folded).
Wheelbase, 80in; 86in (2.03m; 2.18m).
Ground clearance, 8.5in (22cm).
Weight, (unladen) 3,135lb (1,422kg), (laden) 4,510lb (2,046kg).

Performance
Maximum speed, (road) 55mph (88.5kph); (cross country) 15mph (24kph).
Range of action, 217 miles; 435 miles (349km; 700km).
Approach angle, 36⁰.
Departure angle, 47⁰.
Fording depth, 24in (61cm).

Right: Air-portability can be achieved in all sorts of ways. Here a Land Rover and trailer is slung under a Chinook helicopter. *(BM)*